Scandinavian Country Inns & Manors

CLARE & KAREN BROWN

Illustrated by

BARBARA TAPP

TRAVEL PRESS San Mateo, California

Illustrations, Cover Design & Painting: Barbara Tapp
Maps: Keitn Cassell

TRAVEL PRESS editors: Clare Brown, CTC, Karen Brown,
June Brown, CTC, Iris Sandilands; distribution: Kimberly Brown

This book is written as a publication for:

Town and Country Travel Service
16 East Third Avenue, San Mateo, California 94401

International Standard Book Number: 0-930328-21-3
Library of Congress Catalog Card Number: 87-50254
Printed in the United States of America

Travel Press San Mateo, California

Distributed in the United States by:

MACMILLAN PUBLISHING COMPANY

Distributed in Canada by:

COLLIER MACMILLAN CANADA, INC

With Love To

Our Little Alexandra

and

Her Daddy

Contents

HOTEL SECTION

INDEXES

Foreword

"Scandinavian Country Inns and Manors" is written with two main objectives: to describe the most beguiling small hotels throughout Denmark, Finland, Norway and Sweden and to incorporate these very special hotels into itineraries that include sufficient details for you to plan your own holiday. If you love to explore seldom-travelled country lanes, discover isolated hamlets and stay in charming small country inns - then we have done your homework for you. Months of research were spent in finding small hotels with special appeal and in designing itineraries encompassing the most interesting sightseeing. As in our other guides, each of the hotels included has been personally visited to guarantee the quality and each of the itineraries has been "run" to be sure it really works. We feel that "Scandinavian Country Inns and Manors" fills a void in the travel guide market. There are very few books available providing itineraries exploring the countryside in Scandinavia and even fewer books describing charming olde-worlde hotels. So, for those of you who love to travel as we do - the inn way - we again provide you with exquisite little hideaways and fabulous sightseeing suggestions.

"Irish Country Inns and Cottages" will soon be released bringing to eleven the books in our series which now includes: "Austrian Country Inns & Castles", "English, Welsh & Scottish Country Inns", "French Country Inns & Chateaux", "German Country Inns & Castles", "Italian Country Inns & Villas", "Portuguese Country Inns & Pousadas", "Scandinavian Country Inns & Manors", "Spanish Country Inns & Paradors", "Swiss Country Inns & Villas", and our travel cookbook, "European Country Cuisine - Romantic Inns and Recipes". We greatly appreciate your response to each of our guides and through your excellent letters of critique, we are able to improve each new edition. Thank you for sharing your experiences with us.

Introduction

Bergen

Denmark, Finland, Norway and Sweden hold a treasure chest of delights for the tourist: sensational scenery, spotless inns, orderly farms, fascinating stave churches, dramatic castles, mighty glaciers, awesome tunnels, magnificent fjords, delicious meals, spectacular train rides, fabulous boat trips, and above all else - the gracious Scandinavian people. Their friendliness, warmth of welcome and ability to speak English make visitors to their countries feel instantly at home. So join us in exploring not only the well-known tourist delights of Copenhagen, Stockholm, Helsinki, Oslo and Bergen but also off-the-beaten-track itineraries that explore the countryside by car, boat and train, suggesting a charming hotel for each night's stay. Our accommodation section offers a wealth of possibilities: a tiny inn on the windmill-studded island of Oland, a cozy sod-roofed farmhouse in the narrow Boverdalen Valley, a romantic little villa in Finland's lakeland, an exquisite castle overlooking Sweden's Lake Vadstena, a small hotel tucked at the very tip of an enchanting fjord, a cozy thatched-roof hotel in a quaint Danish village. These and many more adventures await you in Scandinavia.

CLOTHING

Dress in Scandinavia is fairly casual: except in the fancier restaurants, a coat and tie are not necessary. Travel light, so that packing and unpacking will not be a chore. As a basic wardrobe the following should meet your needs:

WOMEN: Sturdy low-heeled walking shoes, a pair of "heels" for evening, slacks, a skirt, blouse, several sweaters that can be used in a "layered" effect, raincoat (with removable lining), gloves, scarf or warm hat, overcoat in winter.

MEN: Two pairs of comfortable shoes, two pairs of slacks, a sport coat, a tie, two wash-and-dry dress shirts, several knit shirts, several sweaters, raincoat with removable lining, gloves, warm hat, overcoat in winter.

CREDIT CARDS

Credit cards are often accepted only in major hotels. In the hotel descriptions we indicate what the hotels accept with the following: AX = American Express, VS = Visa, MC = Mastercard (called Eurocard in Europe), DC = Diners Club.

CURRENCY

DENMARK: The currency is Kroner or DKK. At publication $1 was DKK 7.00

FINLAND: The currency is Markkaa or FIM. At publication $1 was FIM 4.70

NORWAY: The currency is Kroner or NOK. At publication $1 was NOK 7.10

SWEDEN: The currency is Kroner or SEK. At publication $1 was SEK 6.57

DRIVING

The penalties for driving under the influence of alcohol are very severe. The use of seatbelts is compulsory. You can drive for a period of up to three months on your local driving license though it is preferred that you obtain an international driver's license. Gasoline is very expensive.

DENMARK: The speed limit is 60-100 kilometers per hour. The roads are excellent, flat and usually very straight.

FINLAND: The speed limit is 60-120 kilometers per hour. Headlights must be on, even during the daylight hours. Sound your horn only in an emergency.

NORWAY: The speed limit is 50-90 kilometers per hour. There are very few expressways and driving in the countryside is often on narrow roads, but the traffic is usually light. In fjord country, roads frequently deadend at a dock where a ferry is the only means to cross to the other side. When driving on back roads, it is sometimes difficult to find gas stations open on Sunday.

SWEDEN: The speed limit is 50-110 kilometers per hour. Headlights must always be on, even in the daylight hours. The roads are excellent though congested in and around Stockholm, especially during commute hours.

ROAD SIGNS: Before starting on the road, prepare yourself by learning the international driving signs so that you can obey all the rules of the road and avoid the embarrassment of heading the wrong way down a small street or parking in a forbidden zone. There are several basic sign shapes. The triangular signs warn that there is danger ahead. The circular signs indicate compulsory rules and information. The square signs give information concerning telephones, parking, camping, etc.

Roisheim Hotel
Lom, Norway

ELECTRICITY

The voltage is 220 volt AC in cycles from 50 to 60. The prongs on plugs vary, making adapters necessary. If in doubt, check at the front desk of your hotel before using any electrical appliances.

FOOD AND DRINK

Throughout Scandinavia you will find eating a pleasure. Great pride is taken in preparing hearty, simple fare from fresh ingredients. The menu always includes fish (the sea, lakes or rivers are never far away), and a selection of delicious cheeses. Reindeer meat and tongue are considered great delicacies. Desserts are especially wonderful: delicious pastries, marvelous thin pancakes, fruit tarts (a particular favorite is the delicious cloudberry) and lots of whipped cream make dieting an impossibility for all but the most disciplined.

Common to all of Scandinavia are two very special treats. The first is the famous open-faced sandwiches, called "smorgas" in Sweden and "smorrebrod" in Denmark. These are meals in themselves and as beautiful as they are delicious. The second treat is Scandinavian breakfast: the table groans with all kinds of fabulous breads, delicious brown crackers, fruits, cheeses, cereals, pate, jams, yogurts, boiled eggs, ham, beef and sausages. If you want to pack a picnic lunch, ask your host if you can be billed for preparing yourself some sandwiches from the morning buffet. This is a very common practice and the hotel will gladly fill your thermos with coffee to complete your meal.

Scandinavian beer is very popular and exceptionally tasty. Be selective though when ordering because certain beers (particularly some of the Danish varieties) have a very high alcohol content and are deliciously deceiving. Other well-known Scandinavian drinks are aquavit (a powerful beverage made from potatoes), vodka and various fruit liqueurs.

In Denmark bottles of liquor can be purchased in a variety of shops, but in the rest of Scandinavia liquor is sold only in government stores which are frequently few and far between - especially in Norway. So, if you like to carry a bottle for your nightcap, remember to purchase it before you leave a major city.

HOTELS

The hotel section is divided by country and the hotels appear alphabetically by town name. We have indicated what each hotel has to offer and described the setting so that you can make the choice to suit your own preferences. We feel if you know what to expect, you will not be disappointed: hotels do not pay to be in this guide so we can be candid and honest in our appraisals. In Finland there are so few country inns that we have included some whose decor is less than perfect. In areas where we needed a hotel choice, we chose the best available and described it as accurately as possible. We have personally inspected all the hotels and stayed in a great many of them.

Scandinavia offers hotels to satisfy every traveller - weathered old farmhouses, cozy thatched-roofed cottages, antique-filled convents, tiny castles, stately manors, posting stations, and charming inns overlooking the sea.

RATES

In choosing a hotel, price will not be a factor for some of you if the hotel is outstanding, while for others budget will guide your choices, so we have included hotels in all price categories. City hotels are costly, but no more so than in other metropolitan areas elsewhere in the world. The hotels in the countryside are much more reasonable although rarely inexpensive. Rates constantly creep upward so that what we quote today will soon be inaccurate. However, to give you an idea of cost we have quoted, in local currency, the price of a superior room for two persons, high season, including breakfast. Each hotel will have some less expensive rooms and also more deluxe accommodation. If you are on a budget, ask the hotel if they have a room without a private bathroom.

RESERVATIONS

People often ask, "Do I need a hotel reservation?" The answer really depends upon how flexible you want to be, how tight your schedule is, which season you are travelling and how disappointed you would be if your first choice is unavailable.

Hotels are frequently completely sold out in major tourist cities during the peak season of June through September. There is less of a problem with space outside the major cities, but during July and August the small inns in the country are also frequently full. You will sometimes find that even in the "off season" there is no space at small inns which are filled to capacity with a group that has come for a seminar. So, if you have your heart set on some special little inn, you should certainly reserve as soon as your travel dates are firm.

Reservations are confining. Most hotels will want a deposit to hold your room and frequently refunds are difficult should you change your plans - especially at the last minute. So it is a double bind. Making reservations locks you into a solid framework, but without reservations you might be paying more and staying at less desirable hotels. For those who like the security of each night preplanned so that once you leave home you do not have to worry about where to rest your head each night, there are several options for making reservations which we have listed below.

TRAVEL AGENT: A travel agent can be of great assistance - particularly if your own time is at a premium. A knowledgeable agent can handle all the details of your holiday and "tie" it all together for you into a neat package including hotel reservations, airline tickets, boat tickets, train reservations, ferry schedules, etc. For your airline tickets there usually is no service fee, but travel agencies make a charge for their other services such as hotel reservations, train tickets, ferry reservations, etc. The best advice is to talk with your local agent. Be frank about how much you want to spend and ask what the service charges will be. Although the travel agency in your town might not be familiar with all the little places in this guide - since some of the inns are so small they do not appear in other sources - loan him/her your book: it is written as a guide for travel agents as well as for individual travellers. (Note for travel agents: most of the inns in this guide pay no commission.)

LETTER: If you start early, you can write directly to the hotels for your reservations. There are certainly many benefits to this in that you can be specific as to your exact preferences. It is important to state clearly: number of people in your party, how many rooms, whether you want a private bathroom, date of arrival and date of departure. Also ask the rate per night and the deposit needed. When you receive a reply send the deposit and ask for a receipt. Be sure to spell out the month: do not use numbers since in Europe they reverse our system - e.g. 6/9 means September 6 to a European, not June 9. Mail can be slow so be sure to allow time for a reply. Remember that many of the hotels in this guide are closed during the winter months.

TELEPHONE: One of the most satisfactory ways to make a reservation is to telephone. The cost is minimal if you direct dial and you can have your answer immediately: if space is not available, you can then decide on an alternate. Ask the operator about the best time to call for the lowest rates. Consider the time change and what time it is in Scandinavia so that you call during their business hours. To phone direct, dial 011, the country code (Denmark: 45, Finland: 358, Norway: 47, Sweden: 46), then the telephone number, omitting the first "0" of the local code (in Finland, omit the first "9" of local code.) Follow up your conversation with a letter, enclosing a deposit if requested.

TELEX: If you have access to a telex machine, this is another efficient way to reach a hotel. When a hotel has a telex, the telex number is given under each hotel listing.

U.S. REPRESENTATIVE: Some hotels in Scandinavia have a United States representative through which reservations can be made. Many of these have a toll free telephone number for your convenience. This is an extremely convenient way to secure a reservation. However, if you are on a strict budget, you might find it less expensive to make the reservation yourself since sometimes a representative makes a charge for his service, only reserves the more expensive rooms, or quotes a higher price to protect himself against currency fluctuations and administrative costs. Furthermore, usually only the larger or more expensive hotels can afford the luxury of an overseas representative - so many of the smaller inns must be contacted directly. We mention hotel representatives along with their phone number whenever a hotel has one.

INFORMATION

General and detailed information can be obtained before you go from:

SCANDINAVIAN NATIONAL TOURIST OFFICE
655 Third Avenue
New York, N.Y. 10017
(212) 949-2333

When you are in Scandinavia as soon as you arrive in a town, stop at the tourist office and stock up on their maps and information booklets on what to see and do.

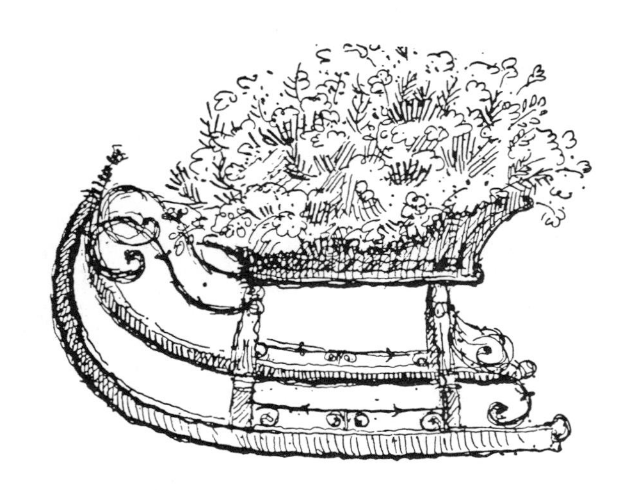

ITINERARIES

The first section of this guide outlines itineraries. You can custom tailor them or combine them to suit your whim and time frame.

The itineraries do not indicate a specific number of nights at each destination, since to do so seemed much too confining. Some travellers like to see as much as possible in a short period of time and do not mind rising with the birds each morning to begin a new adventure. For others, just the thought of packing and unpacking each night makes them shudder in horror and they would never stop for less than three or four nights at any one destination. A third type of tourist does not like to move from hotel to hotel at all: the destination is the focus and they will use this guide to find the "perfect" base for daytime excursions. So use this guide as a reference from which to plan your very own personalized trip. We cannot, however, help adding our recommendation: do not rush. Allow sufficient time during your holiday to settle into a hotel, absorb its special ambiance and to get to know the other guests.

Please note that although a hotel is suggested for each destination in an itinerary, the hotel is just that - a SUGGESTION. Perhaps the hotel seems over your budget, or too fancy, or too simple. Or just not you. If this is the case, each itinerary map indicates by a small star other towns in the area where you can find recommended hotels.

LANGUAGE

One of the joys of travelling in Scandinavia is that you can so easily communicate since English is spoken almost everywhere - except in the Finnish countryside. Even little children learn English in school and are eager to try their skills. But, although the Scandinavians speak English, pick up a small phrase book before you leave home because it is always appreciated if you can say a few words such as "thank you" and "good morning".

MAPS

Our itinerary and hotel location maps are artist's renderings, so our suggestion is to purchase a comprehensive set of both city maps and regional maps before your departure. Then with a highlight pen mark your own "customized" itinerary and pinpoint your hotels. If you live in a metropolitan area, you should have no problem buying maps. If you cannot find the maps you need, there are some excellent bookstores which specialize in travel. On the East Coast, the Complete Traveller, 199 Madison Avenue, New York, NY 10016, telephone: (212) 685-9007 is an excellent source. On the West Coast, Phileas Fogg's Books & Maps, 87 Stanford Shopping Center, Palo Alto, California 94304, telephone: (415) 327-1754 is highly recommended. Both bookstores fill telephone orders.

PASSPORTS

Visas are not needed for tourists staying less than three months. A valid passport is all that is required.

SHOPPING

Most stores are open from 9:00 am or 9:30 am to 5:00 pm or 5:30 pm Monday through Friday, close at 1:00 or 2:00 pm on Saturday and are closed on Sunday.

Shopping is a special pleasure because most of the major cities have shopping streets for pedestrian traffic where you can browse through beautiful stores filled with exquisite merchandise temptingly displayed. The following are some of the items offered for sale:

DENMARK: Amber jewelry, handmade pipes, furniture, Georg Jensen silver, Royal Copenhagen porcelain, Holmegaard glassware, Lego bricks, antiques, fabrics, handknit sweaters, needlework

FINLAND: Fashion goods, gorgeous handwoven fabrics, kitchenware, furs, handwoven rugs, wooden toys, handmade candles, crystal, porcelain, kitchenware, jewelry, knitwear, Marimekko fashions and fabrics, furniture, specialty sauna supplies

NORWAY: Beautiful handknit sweaters, pewter, silver, enamelware, furs, ceramics, textiles, folk-painted wooden items, skis, crystal, wood carvings

SWEDEN: Crystal, cut glass, kitchen gadgets, Dalarna handpainted wooden horses, skis, handicrafts, textiles, porcelain, silverplate, toys, furniture, antiques, lithographs, Carl Larsson prints

Prices in Scandinavia are not inexpensive, but the quality is high. Many shops that cater to tourists display a sticker in the window saying "TAX FREE". This means that they participate in a program that entitles overseas visitors to the refund of VAT (value added tax). To qualify, you need to make a minimum purchase, show your passport and fill in the back of the receipt. Show the goods and the receipt at the special desk as you leave the country and a refund will be processed. If you mail your purchase home, the VAT is subtracted at the time of purchase.

TIPPING

A service charge is almost always added to restaurant and hotel bills. You can add a little something extra for special services rendered, but it is not expected. In Finland taxi drivers do not expect a tip but in Denmark and Norway a few additional kroner are in order, especially if the driver assists with the luggage. In Sweden, drivers are tipped about 10-15% of the fare.

TRANSPORTATION

The transportation system is superb: trains run right on time, buses connect like clockwork with ferry arrivals, subways lace many of the major cities and ships slip constantly back and forth between the countries. Often the transportation itself adds to the fun: quaint little boats thread the Gota Canal, hydrofoils whisk deep into Norway's fjords, coastal steamers cut across the Arctic Circle to the very north of Norway's rugged coastline, colorful red trains take you from the fjord at Flam across dramatic mountains to Mydral and a toy-like steam train puffs between Mariefred and Laggesta. These and other flavorful trips are described in detail in the itineraries "Highlights of Scandinavia by Boat and Train", "Norway's Colorful Coastal Steamer" and "Fantastic Fjords of Norway - Daytrips from Bergen".

There are several travel bargains available for persons using public transportation. If you are travelling all over Europe, the "Eurailpass" offers unlimited travel by first class train through 16 countries. The Eurailpass has a wide variety of choices from fifteen days to three months, each an excellent value if you plan to do much travel by train. If you plan to travel totally within Scandinavia, there is an even better value, the "Scandinavian Railpass" which can be bought at any rail station in Scandinavia and is valid for unlimited travel on the railroads of Denmark, Finland, Norway and Sweden. These passes are valid for 21 days and offered in either first or second class. The Scandinavian Railpass also gives a 50% reduction on certain ferries between countries. In addition, Denmark, Finland, Norway and Sweden each offer rail passes.

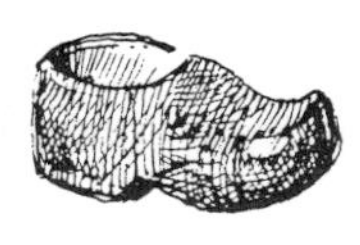

WEATHER

Scandinavia covers such a large geographic area, reaching from the far north of the Arctic Circle to south of the 55th parallel, that it is impossible to generalize on the weather. You can never be sure of what to expect so even in summer always carry along a raincoat and warm sweater. We have included some average temperatures and rainfall to help you in planning your holiday:

DENMARK: Average daily temperature: Copenhagen - January 32°F, July 64°F. The wettest month is usually August, the driest February.

FINLAND: Average daily temperature: Helsinki - January 26°F, July 71°F. The wettest month is usually July, the driest February and March.

NORWAY: Average daily temperature: Oslo - January 25°F, July 64°F. While Bergen averages 75 inches of rain a year Oslo has only 29 inches. The wettest month is usually October, the driest June.

SWEDEN: Average daily temperature: Stockholm - January 27°F, July 63°F. The wettest month is usually August, the driest February.

It is difficult to plan exactly the best time of year to travel to Scandinavia. If you enjoy winter sports, naturally winter would be the season to visit the ski resorts of Norway, Sweden and Finland. Otherwise spring through fall is recommended. Although you can never depend on the fickle weather, late spring is often one of the drier seasons and especially beautiful. In summertime the days in Scandinavia are very long and above the Arctic Circle it is light for 24 hours a day - the further north you go, the longer the period of the "midnight sun". Conversely, in winter the days are very short and above the Arctic Circle there are times when the sun never rises.

Highlights of Scandinavia by Train & Boat

Highlights of Scandinavia by Train & Boat

"Highlights of Scandinavia by Train & Boat" is a captivating itinerary, but, because of the size of Scandinavia, a very long one. Those with the luxury of time can follow the suggested routing in its entirety, savoring the spectacular mood and beauty of Scandinavia. However, since many travellers have a limited time they can be away from home, this itinerary has been carefully planned so that it can be segmented. You can customize your own itinerary by choosing the part that most appeals to you or covers a portion of Scandinavia you have missed on previous trips. For example, you could begin the itinerary in Bergen, meander through glorious fjords, enjoy one of the most scenic train rides in the world and end your trip in Oslo. Or, perhaps, start in Helsinki, take the ferry through spectacular archipelagos to Stockholm and then weave your way across the serenely beautiful heartland of Sweden by a quaint steamer to Gothenburg. But, whether you can meander through every city and hamlet or only choose a limited segment, you are in for a treat. Scandinavia is gorgeous.

Gota Canal

Scandinavia lends itself beautifully to travel without a car. In fact, in many places a car be a hindrance: Norway's coast is so riddled with fjords that by boat is really THE way to travel and in some cases the only way to reach a village. So leave the car behind and enjoy the spectacular scenery, and instead of watching the road savor the glorious mountains and fjords. Public transport in Scandinavia is admirably synchronized - the boat pulls up to the harbor as the train is about to leave from the adjacent station, the ferry chugs into the dock just as the connecting boat is ready to leave - it is a joy to travel. Language is not a problem: almost everyone speaks English, so if you have a question, you can readily find the answer.

There is one prerequisite to this itinerary: you MUST travel light. Walk a short distance with your luggage before you go - if you are exhausted, you are taking too much. Bring just one small suitcase per person. Pack some warm clothes and leave your dressy ones behind. If you only feel comfortable travelling with all of your favorite clothes, you can still enjoy this itinerary, but follow it by car instead of public transport.

Note: The schedules are given only to provide a basic outline. It is extremely important that you check the most current schedules for the period you want to travel. Not only might the times vary, but also many of the trains and ferries operate only in the summer. In addition to reconfirming the departure times, make as many of the reservations as possible before leaving home to save yourself time and aggravation. Almost all of the trains can be reserved in advance and seats confirmed in first class. Many of the ferries can also be reserved in advance and need to be if you want to be assured of a private cabin (such as on the journey between Sweden and Finland). The Gota Canal boats and the Norwegian Coastal steamers are so popular in summer that many of the passengers book almost a year in advance. Plan ahead for the most carefree holiday. On the last page of this itinerary information is given on where to call to make reservations. The Scandinavian National Tourist Office (see page 9) can also give you information.

This itinerary begins in BERGEN, definitely one of the most charming cities in Norway, or, for that matter, in all of Europe. If you arrive by plane you will be initiated into the wonders to come as the plane sweeps low over crystal clear water dotted with miniature islands where boats nestle in tiny coves. After clearing customs (a most civilized system of "nothing to declare" or "duty"), you will find a bus into town with departures coordinating with arrivals of all flights. The bus stops first at the bus depot in Bergen and then goes on to the SAS ROYAL HOTEL. The SAS Royal is a lovely large deluxe hotel cleverly incorporating the medieval wooden buildings along the Bryggen (the Wharf). If you want the finest accommodations, stay here, but since this itinerary continues on to the Sognefjord, the AUGUSTIN HOTEL is the most convenient place to stay as it is only a three-minute walk to the dock from which the express ferries leave.

The Augustin is a simple small hotel, beautifully located and with friendly management. There are a few choice rooms with a view of the harbor. If you book far enough in advance, you might be able to secure one of these. Especially well positioned are the corner rooms on the upper floors.

Allow several days to explore Bergen - no better way than on foot. The fjord reaches its finger into the middle of the city which climbs the low hills rising from the water. On one side of the harbor lies the colorful section known as Bryggen. This is the old wharf, extremely picturesque, with brightly colored wooden buildings dating from the Hanseatic period lining the wharf and reflecting in the water. Recently these inviting old buildings have become a tourist attraction, with little boutiques, restaurants and galleries built into the shells of the old dwellings. At the tip of the finger of the Bergenfjord is the Outdoor Market. Here flower stalls, brilliant with color, share space with fishermen selling all kinds of fresh fish artfully displayed beneath canopied tables. The main shopping street of Bergen is the Strandgaten, a two-minute walk from the market place. This is a pedestrian mall with many stores selling souvenirs, including a wide choice of beautiful handknitted Norwegian sweaters. (The stores close on Saturdays about 1:30 pm and reopen on Monday.)

Augustin Hotel
Bergen

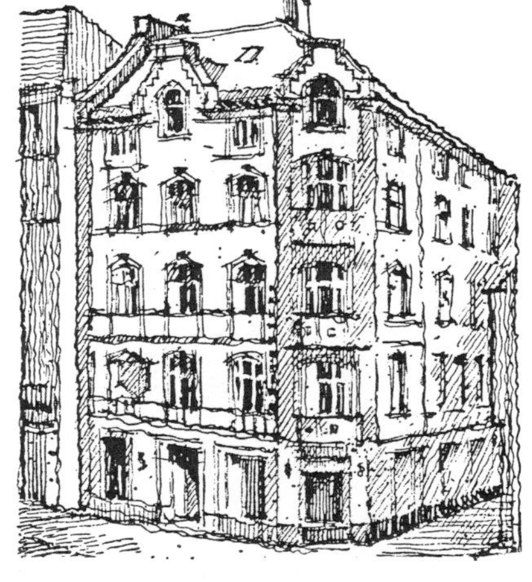

The most efficient way to plan your sightseeing is to pay a visit to the tourist office located in the center of town. It offers a wealth of free information plus a variety of inexpensive maps and special booklets with detailed information on sightseeing. You can purchase tickets for sightseeing here and most of the tour buses conveniently depart just across the street.

Whether you take a tour bus or go sightseeing individually, you will want to include the following sights. The HANSEATIC MUSEUM is housed in one of Bergen's old wooden buildings - its interior gives a glimpse of what it was like to live in that period. The MARITIME MUSEUM is a modern museum tracing the development of shipping from the Old Norse period to the modern day. The

ROSENKRANTZ TOWER is a dramatic 13th-century royal residence which was also used as a fort. The BERGEN AQUARIUM is the largest in Scandinavia. OLD BERGEN is an open-air museum with more than 35 18th- and 19th-century wooden houses. BRYGGEN is the wharf dotted with colorful Hanseatic wooden buildings. TROLDHAUGEN is Edvard Grieg's home where he composed many of his best known works, and FANTOFT STAVE CHURCH is a beautiful church nearby. ST MARY'S CHURCH is the oldest building in Bergen and one of the loveliest Romanesque churches in Norway. The ISLAND OF LYSOEN is laced with walking paths and it is here that you find the famous violin virtuoso Ole Bull's villa. But before you begin exhaustive sightseeing, ride the funicular railway to FLOIEN at the top of one of Bergen's seven hills - on a clear day the city is laid before you like a beautiful map. Enjoy the incredible view and plan your sightseeing excursions.

DESTINATION I BALESTRAND Kvikne's Hotel

The SOGNEFJORD EXPRESS FERRY leaves from the pier near the Augustin Hotel. It is advisable to have reservations in advance. If you have sufficient time, you can call or write to: Fylkesbaatane I Sogn og Fjordane, 197 Strandgaten, 5000 Bergen, Norway, telephone (05) 32 40 15. If you have not written ahead, you can go to the ferry office next to the departure pier and buy the tickets when you arrive in Bergen (the office is open only near the times when the boats leave - about 7:00 am or 4:00 pm). Do not oversleep or dawdle at the hotel because your hydrofoil leaves the dock promptly at 7:30 am. You will not have time for the regular breakfast if you are staying at the Augustin Hotel, but ask in advance and they will arrange a Continental breakfast.

7:30 am	leave Bergen by hydrofoil
noon	arrive Balestrand

Your hydrofoil, the M/S Hyen, has a comfortable lounge with three sections of chairs and wide windows providing excellent views. There is space on the upper deck to sit outside in fine weather. If you are hungry, a small snack bar serves sandwiches, cold drinks, coffee, tea and candy.

After leaving the harbor the engines quicken and you are "flying" down the fjord. The boat weaves through the archipelago past tiny islands with brightly hued summer homes, each with its boat dock tucked into the rocks by the water. Briefly the hydrofoil nears the open ocean, but soon darts into the entrance of the Sognefjord and makes a stop at the village of LARVIK where a few passengers sporting stout walking shoes and backpacks disembark and a few more hardy souls clamber aboard. The ferry then dips deeper into the gorgeous Sognefjord where steep mountains rise precipitously from the waters. Occasionally patches of velvet green dotted with farm buildings appear. Look up and you see small farms balanced on high ledges. The houses are similar to those seen on the New England coast - neat little wooden homes, often painted "barn red" with attractive white trim.

About four and a half hours after leaving Bergen, BALESTRAND appears in the distance. It is easy to spot the KVIKNE'S HOTEL - a marvelous Victorian gingerbread building dating from 1887 - for it dominates a small peninsula that juts into the fjord. Alight quickly as the ferry stops for only a few minutes. It is a short walk up the path to the Kvikne's Hotel, perched on a knoll above the harbor.

There are two sections to Kvikne's Hotel - the new wing is quite modern with nice bedrooms and lovely views; the original part of the hotel has some nice rooms whose large balconies afford blissful views of the fjord. The Kvikne's Hotel is big and quite commercial with busloads of tourists, but it is also quite unique, being one of the largest wooden buildings in Europe. Also, although large, the hotel remains very personal. The Kvikne family has owned the hotel for many generations.

Kvikne's Hotel
Balestrand

There are many excursions available in Balestrand. Apart from the obvious outings such as beautiful walks or bicycle rides, there are also day excursions that are sold at the tourist office located in a building near the pier. One tour you should not miss is by ferry up a gorgeous little fjord to see the JOSTEDALS GLACIER. The ferry leaves only steps from where your hydrofoil arrived from Bergen. The ferry pulls away from the dock and makes its way up a narrow fjord to the tiny town of FJAERLAND where a bus meets the boat at the pier and takes the passengers to the Jostedals Glacier where there is time allowed to explore on foot and also to have a snack at the small cafe. Not only is it interesting to see the glacier, but the boat ride on the splendid Fjaerlandfjord is glorious - worth the outing even if there were no majestic as its prize.

Another very special excursion is to visit the 13th-century HOPPERSTAD STAVE CHURCH. The first leg of the tour is by a ferry whch leaves from the pier below the hotel. The ferry crosses the fjord where the bus is waiting for the short ride to the Hopperstad stave church, which is not only an outstanding example of a stave church, but is also picturesquely situated in a lovely meadow, surrounded in spring by wildflowers.

Allow a few days in Balestrand so that you can soak in the beauty of the fjords and make several day excursions. When it is time to leave, a new adventure in beauty awaits you.

12:05 pm leave Balestrand by ferry
1:50 pm arrive Flam

The express ferry continues deeper into the Sognefjord (the longest fjord in Norway) until reaching a smaller branch called the Aurlandsfjord. About 15 minutes after taking this side fjord, the ferry slows down and you notice another large car ferry waiting ahead. Then quite a remarkable transaction occurs: the two boats pull side by side and a ramp is slid across the gap betwen them. Passengers quickly pass back and forth and immediately both ferries are on their way again. The boat ferry then heads down one narrow branch of the Aurlandsfjord, toward the town of Gudvangen, and your boat, the Neroy, heads down another narrow fork toward FLAM. The journey is lovely, with steep mountains, glaciers in the distance, lush, velvety green patches of farmland. But as you now head down the narrow fjord the excitement increases as the giant cliffs plunge into the bottle green water. At times the hills seem almost to form walls of solid rock closing in the fjord; frequently waterfalls cascade angrily down the steep embankments. Soon you see the head of the fjord and the tiny town of Flam. As you approach the pier, notice how conveniently the Norwegians plan their transportation system - a bright red train is waiting a few steps away to pick up passengers from the boat.

There is a train for MYDRAL at 2:55 pm, but, for the best connection to Oslo, dawdle in Flam and take the 3:25 pm train, giving you time for lunch and a walk. The general store in the plaza sells picnic supplies and the nearby FRETHEIM

HOTEL serves an excellent lunch. Should you wish to overnight in Flam, the Fretheim is a good choice.

3:25 pm leave Flam by train
4:10 pm arrive Mydral

Be sure to be at the station on time because the train pulls away on the dot. Allow time to stop at the information booth next to the train and pick up a brochure that describes the FLAM - MYDRAL RAILWAY. As the train chugs up the 1,845-foot ascent from Flam to Mydral it negotiates 20 tunnels with a total length of 3.7 miles - a great feat of engineering. The steep gradient is unique for standard trains; but do not be nervous, for there are five braking systems on the train - any one of which is sufficient to stop it. However, you probably won't be thinking of such mundane matters as safety with the spectacular scenery displayed at every turn. On the first leg of the journey, the train follows a crystal clear mountain river through a lush, narrow mountain valley with walls of granite. As the train climbs into the mountains, the scenery becomes ever harsher but even more dramatic, with furious waterfalls leaping from the cliffs. The conductor announces places of special interest along the way and tells you which side of the train they will be seen on so that you can dash from side to side with your camera to capture the beauty. The train conveniently slows when it comes to outstanding vistas and even stops briefly for photographs of the Kjosfossen waterfall. All too soon the journey ends and you are at the end of the line in Mydral. Soon your train for Oslo approaches, the station agent announces its arrival and everyone crosses to track 2 to board it. There is a sign by the ticket office showing the formation of the train so that you can stand at the appropriate spot to be ready to board your car. (Seat reservations are necessary.)

5:07 pm leave Mydral by train
10:00 pm arrive Oslo

The scenery is bleakly dramatic for about an hour after leaving Mydral: mostly rock with cold gray lakes and mountain grass struggling to survive near the distant glaciers. As the train nears the ski village of GEILO the scenery becomes softer - lakes and forests appear, and farm villages nestle on the mountainsides. Your train, the "Bergen Express", has meal service, so you dine leisurely as you pass through gorgeous scenery, arriving in Oslo just in time to take a cab to the hotel and get a good night's sleep.

An excellent hotel choice in Oslo is the sophisticated, charming HOTEL CONTINENTAL, a fairly large hotel built in the grand style at the turn of the century. The Hotel Continental is centrally located between the Royal Palace and the National Theater - perfect for sightseeing. The harbor with the tour boats is only a two-minute walk away; the subway station is just across the street; the buses leave from the corner; the garden parkway running through the center of Stockholm is steps away; and the main shopping street, Karl Johansgate, is an easy stroll away. In other words, all of Oslo is at your command - either by boat, bus, subway or on foot.

Hotel Continental
Oslo

Founded by King Harald Hardraada in the 11th century, OSLO is the largest city in Norway and yet has the advantages of "country living". Only minutes from the heart of the city you can be skiing in the mountains, camping in the forests, sailing on the fjords, or relaxing on the beach - the Norwegians love nature and in Oslo the outdoors is right at hand.

There are sightseeing bus tours leaving both mornings and afternoons from in front of the City Hall (located across the street from the central harbor). However, since so many of the sights in Oslo are within walking distance of your hotel or easily accessible by public transportation, you might want to explore on your own. Karl Johansgate, a pedestrian street, runs through the center of town and offers the opportunity to browse through dozens of stores displaying gorgeous handknit sweaters, hats and gloves, and souvenirs, or to stop for a coffee in one of the outdoor cafes. At one end of the Karl Johansgate is the ROYAL PALACE, with a red flag waving from the roof when the king is in residence, and at the other end is the East Train Terminal. OSLO CATHEDRAL is a 17th-century building with beautiful stained glass windows and medieval pulpit and altar. The CITY HALL (located only a block from the Hotel Continental) is a new building with a series of giant murals depicting modern-day Norway with an emphasis on the recent turmoils of the Second World War and the growth of Norway, stressing the importance of the family as the heart of the country. The AKERSHUB CASTLE is seen on the bluff overlooking the harbor. This castle houses the NORWEGIAN RESISTANCE MUSEUM which depicts the inspiring bravery of the Norwegians during World War II. The NATIONAL THEATER faces the park across the street from your hotel. In front of the theater large statues of Norway's literary giants, Ibsen and Bjornson, flank the entrance.

A wonderful day can be spent on the BYGDOYA PENINSULA which juts into the harbor. You can take either the ferry or bus, but, if the weather is pleasant, a combination of the two makes a delightful excursion. Take the number 30 bus from behind the National Theater and tell the bus driver you want to get off at the NORWEGIAN FOLK MUSEUM. This is an enormous park of buildings brought from all over Norway and reconstructed to show life in Norway from medieval times. It is especially interesting because all types of buildings are shown, from the simplest farmhouse to splendid homes of the wealthy. Not only homes, but shops, pharmacies and a stave church are reconstructed. There are several museums in the park and many of the buildings are furnished appropriate to the era in which they were built. When you buy your entrance ticket ask for a map of the whole peninsula. This will show you where all the sights are located.

After leaving the Folk Museum, turn to the right and then around the corner and you are soon at the most fascinating museum in Oslo - the VIKING MUSEUM. Here you will see three Viking ships, two of which are in remarkably good condition. They were found in burial sites where the condition of the clay soil worked as a preservative. As you look at these ships, the wonder of the impertinent bravery of the Vikings who took these vulnerable ships throughout the world - even to America - awes you. The beauty of the ships' sleek and lovely lines is astounding. Wonderful Viking sleds are also artfully displayed. It is about a 20-minute walk (well marked and mostly downhill) from the Viking Museum to the KON-TIKI MUSEUM which is located at the harbor. Along the waterfront are several very interesting naturical museums: one building houses the fragile Kon-Tiki which made its way across the Pacific from Peru to Polynesia (proving the possibility that Easter Island could indeed have been discovered by South Americans in small boats). Another building contains the Flam, a famous boat which explored the inhospitable polar waters. Adjacent to the Flam and Kon-Tiki museums is the pier where every 30 minutes, on the hour and half hour, a boat zips back to Oslo's central harbor.

Another outing easily taken by public transport is to the FROGNER PARK. Take the subway from behind the National Theater, to the Frogner stop. When you buy your ticket ask the ticket agent and he will give you a map of the stops. Frogner Park is most famous for the 650 modern sculptures by the controversial artist, Gustav Vigeland. A large monolith surrounded by a series of statues in white stone depicts all phases of life, but more appealing are the realistically sculpted statues that surround the largest fountain in Scandinavia. These statues, especially the ones of small children, are delightfully whimsical. In addition to the statues, the 75-acre park has beautiful rose gardens, inviting shade trees, small lakes and rolling lawns. It is fun to watch the pretty young mothers pushing baby carriages while blond children romp beside them.

If the weather is clear and you enjoy spectacular views, visit the HOLMENKOLLEN SKI JUMP - another easy do-it-yourself tour. Take the subway that leaves from behind the National Theater (there are two subway stations adjacent to each other - you can ask at the entrance which is the correct one for Holmenkollen). Although located in a modern station, the old-fashioned wooden streetcar is a delight. The first part of the journey is underground and then the quaint little trolley pops into the open and slowly climbs through the city and up the mountain. Get off at the next-to-last exit (about a 30-minute ride) at the HOLMENKOLLEN STATION. A path leads upward for the 10-minute walk to the Holmenkollen Ski Jump, used only a few days a year for skiing but with breathtaking views. If you time your visit with a mealtime, you can dine and enjoy the view at either the HOLMENKOLLEN CAFE or the intriguing Viking-style HOLMENKOLLEN PARK HOTEL.

Farther afield, but also feasible as a day trip from Oslo, is an excursion to FREDRIKSTAD. For this adventure, take the train from Oslo to Fredrikstad (the 9:00 am train arrives at 10:30 am). The train journey is not too interesting, but have faith, because just a few blocks from the Fredrikstad station, a ferry leaves for the few-minute ride to the ISLAND OF FREDRIKSTAD, the most perfectly preserved small fortified city in Norway. Enjoy wandering through the 17th-century fortress, the museum, the church and the arts and crafts center. Several restaurants are available for lunch before taking the short ferry ride back again for the afternoon train back to Oslo (there are several trains leaving in the afternoon for your return - a convenient suggestion would be the 3:06 pm train which arrives in Oslo at 4:34 pm).

If your time is precious, there is a direct train from Oslo to Stockholm. However, try to squeeze in a day or two in the Swedish countryside by breaking your journey in SVARTA, where you can enjoy an interlude at the romantic SVARTA HERRGARD, a beautiful manor house that faces a lake.

8:55 am	leave Oslo by train
12:59 pm	arrive Degerfors

The ride from Oslo to DEGERFORS is lovely in a gentle way - you pass rolling hills, manicured farms, quiet lakes and many forests. About two hours after leaving Oslo you cross the border into Sweden, but, except for the conductor strolling through to see your tickets, there are no customs formalities.

Svarta Herrgard
Svarta

When you arrive at the Degerfors station, taxis are sometimes waiting. If not, use the taxi phone booth in the parking lot - crank the bell, lift up the receiver, and - magic - a voice asks if you want a taxi. Just say you are at the train station and within moments a cab arrives. It is about a 15-minute drive to the Svarta Herrgard and, at the time this guide was written, the cost each way was SEK 100. After a pleasant drive through the forests, you arrive at the Svarta Herrgard, an attractive manor. It is not until you go inside and look out the rear windows that you can appreciate the hotel's excellent position overlooking the lake, with a grassy lawn running down to the waterfront where chairs and benches are strategically set to capture the view.

The joy of Svarta is that there is nothing to do. Trails beckon you into the forest. Or perhaps take one of the little boats tied at the pier and paddle out into the lake and float about and dream. Fishing is a favorite pastime. If it is raining enjoy a good book. When making reservations ask for a bedroom overlooking the lake - the view is idvllic

DESTINATION IV STOCKHOLM Lady Hamilton Hotel

After an interlude in the countryside continue on to STOCKHOLM.

12:59 pm leave Degefors by train (seat reservations required)
3:30 pm arrive Stockholm

Upon arrival in Stockholm take a taxi to the Old Town to the LADY HAMILTON HOTEL. This is an especially appealing small hotel: antiques are everywhere and each guestroom displays a handpainted cabinet - an authentic example of old Swedish folk art. Other whimsical touches are the little antique rocking horses cleverly displayed throughout the hotel. The building dates from the 1470s, but has been lovingly restored with beautiful taste by the Bengtsson family. There is no formal restaurant in the hotel, but a cheerful coffee room serves snacks.

Lady Hamilton Hotel
Stockholm

Stockholm is spread across 14 islands in the Baltic Sea - it really is one of Europe's most enchanting cities. The oldest part of the town, called GAMLA STAN or Old Town, is located on one of the smallest of the islands. This is certainly one of the most charming parts of Stockholm. Here you find the ROYAL PALACE (open to the public on guided tours) and the 700-year-old STOCKHOLM CATHEDRAL (in the center of the Old Town atop a hill). It is great fun to wander the narrow little streets, browse through boutiques, stop for a cup of tea in a quaint cafe or discover a fabulous tiny restaurant.

A short walk across a bridge takes you from the Old Town to the "New". The majestic GRAND HOTEL faces the harbor where the dock in front of the hotel is lined with boats, each with a sign in front explaining which sightseeing tour they operate. Probably no other city has such a fascinating selection of boat tours available: UNDER THE BRIDGES OF STOCKHOLM criss-crosses back and forth under Stockholm's many bridges, ARCHIPELAGO CRUISE takes you through the archipelago, DROTTNINGHOLM goes to the 17th-century Drottningholm Palace, residence of the Royal Family, and also to see the 18th-century theater nearby, VAXHOLM takes you by boat to Vaxholm, a nearby yachting center, with time for lunch and shopping before returning to Stockholm.

A daytrip to UPPSALA can be taken on a bus tour, but this stunning old city can also be reached independently. To do it on your own, take the M/S SKOKLOSTER from the harbor at 9:45 am (ask at the tourist office for the correct pier), arriving in SIGTUNA at 12:15 pm. Sigtuna, dating back to the 11th century, is one of Sweden's most charming villages. You may want to end your boat ride here, have lunch and return on the 3:30 pm boat to Stockholm. However, the M/S Skokloster continues on to ROSERSBERG PALACE, a royal palace since 1757. Here you can sightsee and transfer to the 4:00 pm boat - arriving in Uppsala at 5:30 pm. Uppsala is a 700-year-old university town of beautiful medieval buildings set on twisting streets by a river. Explore the town, have dinner, then take one of trains that frequently run to Stockholm.

If you are travelling with children, or if the child in you loves quaint boats and trains, take a day's excursion to MARIEFRED. (Ask at the central tourist office in Stockholm to verify times and reservation procedures.) The journey is like a Disneyland adventure. First you travel by a quaint little steamboat to the idyllic hamlet of Mariefred, one of Sweden's most attractive little villages. As you chug up to the dock, you will see the GRIPSHOLMS VARDSHUS adjacent to the harbor. This is an excellent place to eat lunch. After a snack, follow the path around the lake to GRIPSHOLM CASTLE. This fabulous castle, on its own little island, exhibits Europe's largest collection of portraits. After visiting the castle, retrace your steps to the harbor and board the quaint little vintage "toy" train for the short ride to LAGGESTA where you connect with the modern train which whisks you back to Stockholm.

An overnight boat excursion (leaving at 9:30 am) is available which winds through the inner islands of Stockholm and then enters the Stromma Canal to SANDHAMN, a summer resort famous as the home of the Royal Swedish Yacht Club. This 17th-century village with its closely huddled houses and narrow lanes has a simple hotel, the SANDHAMN, where you overnight before returning to Stockholm the next day on the 6:00 pm boat.

DESTINATION V HELSINKI Hotel Seurahuone Socis

If you have the time, try to squeeze in this round trip excursion to HELSINKI. Helsinki is well worth a visit and you can combine your visit with sightseeing trips into the countryside.

9:15 pm leave Stockholm by ship (Viking Line or Silja Line)
8:00 am arrive Turku (next morning)

The journey across the narrow channel between Sweden and Finland is filled with islands. It seems that no sooner do you leave the archipelago of Stockholm before you find yourself weaving through the archipelago of Helsinki. The Viking Line ships are large and very efficient. If it is summer, long after boarding the sky will be light and you will have time to enjoy the scenery before retiring for the night. The cabins are not expensive, so I certainly suggest one of the best with twin beds and a private bathroom. It will be light early, so you can enjoy the beautiful approach as the ship glides through the tiny islands on its way into the harbor at TURKU.

Instead of choosing Turku as your first port of call in Finland, you can take either the Silja Line or the Viking Line directly to Helsinki - both leave in the evening from Stockholm and arrive in the early morning at Helsinki. But since Turku is an old, very picturesque city, this is a good opportunity to tuck a little more sightseeing into your itinerary.

After docking in Turku, take a cab to the train station and check your luggage at the baggage office to be left until you return in the afternoon to take the train to Helsinki. Turku is a good walking city, but it is always a wise idea to come prepared by bringing with you a city map on which you have marked the following suggested do-it-yourself sightseeing tour. Only a few blocks from the train station, located in a lovely small park, is the MUSEUM OF ART, with a rich collection of paintings and sculpture. About two blocks from the Museum is the heart of Turku, the MARKET SQUARE. On one side of the square is the SWEDISH THEATER dating from 1838 and on another side the ORTHODOX CHURCH dating from about the same period. From the Market Square walk to the AURAJOKI RIVER which weaves picturesquely through the old city. When you reach the river you see the tower of the CATHEDRAL, so you can easily find your way. The Cathedral, a massive Romanesque-style building, dates from 1290. After visiting the Cathedral, visit the nearby HANDICRAFT MUSEUM. The Handicraft Museum is not a normal "museum" but rather a collection of houses which survived the 1827 fire and now house a series of fascinating craft shops. From the Handicraft Museum, return to the river and cross over the bridge at Kaskenkatu Street. As you cross the river, you will see below to the left along the riverbank the TOWN HALL and next to it a wonderful small PHARMACY MUSEUM housed in the oldest surviving wooden house in Turku. Definitely stop in the Pharmacy Museum to see the excellent display of how a pharmacy operated in bygone days and how the family lived in the same shop. Continue walking by the river and cross over to the other side at the next bridge. About a block farther are moored two old sailing ships: the SIGYN (built in 1887) is open to the public in summer.

There are trains leaving Turku for Helsinki at 12:00 noon, 3:45 pm, 5:25 pm (except Saturday) and 8:46 pm. The following suggestion would give you time for some sightseeing and lunch:

3:45 pm leave Turku by train
6:27 pm arrive Helsinki

Upon arrival in Helsinki, you will find the HOTEL SEURAHUONE SOCIS conveniently located just across the street from the train station. Built around the turn of the century, the Seurahuone Socis is one of the few hotels in Helsinki which has an olde-worlde ambiance. In addition to having a very attractive Viennese-style cafe and comfortable guestrooms, this hotel is also superbly located for sightseeing.

Hotel Seurahuone Socis
Helsinki

There are many places of interest in Helsinki, an appealing city founded by King Gustav Vasa in 1550. Most of the sights are within easy walking distance of your hotel. If you prefer to ride, a streetcar leaves from almost in front of the hotel for a 45-minute loop around the city. Along the way, the places of interest are announced by a recording (do not count on understanding too well - the recording is not very clear and the trolley very noisy). Just a few blocks from the hotel is the famous STOCKMAN'S DEPARTMENT STORE. This is the finest department store in Finland and an excellent place to shop for gifts. From Stockman's it is a few minutes' walk to Pohjoiseplandi, the lovely parklike promenade which stretches to the market place by the harbor. Get up early one morning to witness the picturesque market bursting with the brilliant color of the flower stalls. The market, selling flowers, vegetables, fruits, fish and handicrafts, is open Monday through Saturday from 7:00 am to 2:00 pm. From the market square sightseeing boats leave to explore the harbor. One of the most interesting excursions is to the FORTRESS OF SUOMENLINNA, located on an island about a 15-minute ride away. All of the boat excursions post their destinations and the times of departure on the pier.

Other notable sights in Helsinki are: the SIBELIUS MONUMENT, an extremely modern sculpture of pipes honoring Finland's famous composer, Jean Sibelius; the 19th-century SENATE SQUARE where you can see the bronze statue of Czar Alexander II; the SEURASAARI OPEN-AIR MUSEUM where farm and manor houses from all over Finland have been erected; the USPENSKI CATHEDRAL, a majestic church dating from 1868; and the TEMPPELIAUKIO CHURCH, a modern Lutheran church carved out of a rock and dramatically crowned with an enormous copper dome.

One of Finland's greatest attractions is its beautiful countryside dotted with lakes and laced with trees. In order to see some of this delightful scenery, plan to take advantage of some of the excellent tours available from Helsinki. Many of the excursions operate only in the summertime, so hopefully you can plan your holiday accordingly. Most highly recommended is the excursion by boat to the wonderful old town of PORVOO (a colorful village of painted wooden buildings which shares the honor along with Turku of being one of the two oldest towns in Finland). Another tour goes by bus to HAMEENLINNA to visit the 700-year-old CASTLE OF HAME, HATTULA MEDIEVAL CHURCH and the IITTALA GLASSWORKS. A shorter outing, but also very pleasant, is to HVITTRASK, the former studio and residence of three of Finland's most talented architects: Eliel Saarinen, Armas Lindgren and Herman Gesellius.

When it is time to leave Finland, it is a pleasant overnight ferry ride back to Stockholm, passing through the glorious archipelagos of Helsinki and Stockholm.

6:00 pm leave Helsinki by ship (Viking Line or Silja Line)
9:00 am arrive Stockholm (next morning)

When you reach Stockholm, you might want to return to the Lady Hamilton Hotel, but if you enjoy the adventure of new experiences, try the deluxe VICTORY HOTEL (named for Lord Nelson's famous ship). The Bengtsson family owns both hotels so it is not surprising the same exquisite taste prevails in both. The Victory Hotel (opened in 1987) is cleverly incorporated into one of the finest medieval buildings in the Old Town of Stockholm. In addition to the outstanding collection of antiques, the Victory has an excellent restaurant.

Victory Hotel
Stockholm

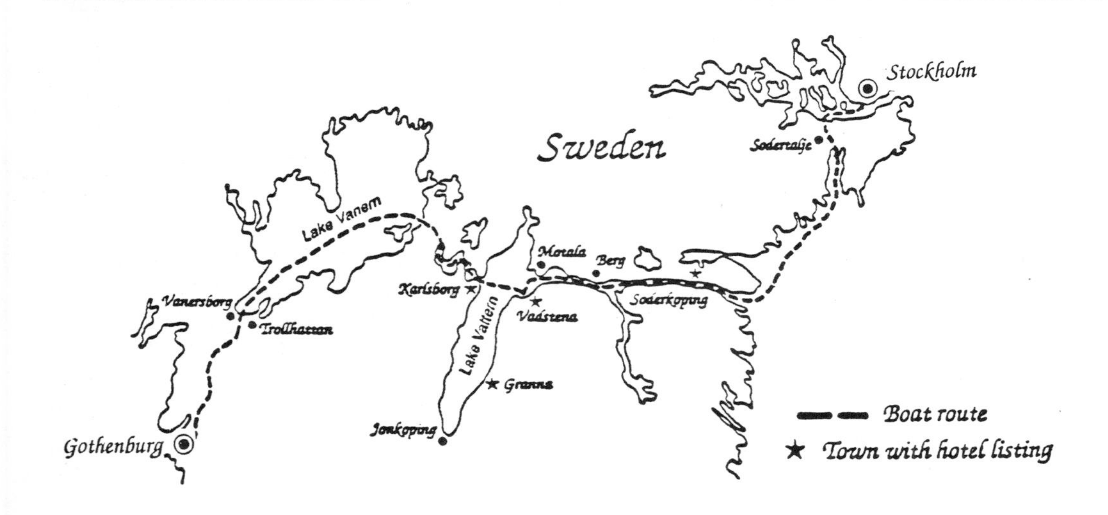

9:00 am leave Stockholm by boat
4:30 pm arrive Gothenburg (arrival is on the third day)

This boat trip through the lakes and canals linking Stockholm and Gothenburg is recommended only for those who can cope with small boats and cramped conditions for three days. However, the journey is very special and therefore included. If, after reading the description, this boat ride does not seem your cup of tea, you can take a train to Gothenburg.

There are three boats on this route: the Juno built in 1847, the Wilhelm Tham built in 1912, and the Diana built in 1931. Each is a funny little old-fashioned wooden affair, wonderfully nostalgic. None of the cabins has a private bathroom - toilets are down the hall and one shower is shared by all. The cabins are ludicrously small (about 6 feet by 5 feet). The lower bed is adequate but the top bunk which pulls down at night is a most uncomfortable board-like pad which hovers precariously close to the lower bed. There is no room for luggage - the best you can hope for is to squeeze a tiny suitcase under the bed. If there are two people travelling, I suggest you splurge and each take a cabin to give yourselves a little more space. The lounge is so small that in bad weather there is not enough room for everyone to share the space. The dining room is one of the most attractive rooms, but the food is not outstanding. But read on. Now that you are aware of the problems, here is what makes this journey absolutely delightful.

MS Diana

The canal itself is a 19th-century engineering feat and encompasses 322 miles between Stockholm and Gothenburg, about one-third of the journey on artificial canals with the remainder on a chain of rivers and lakes. The journey begins at sea level and during the three-day trip a height of over 300 feet is reached while crossing Lake Vattern, before stepping down through a series of locks until sea level is reached again at Gothenburg. In all, the boat passes through 65 locks, the oldest of which dates back to 1813. But it isn't just the fascination of the intricate, old-fashioned lock system (one is still operated by a man standing turning a large wheel) - the trip promises even more. After pulling away from the dock, your little wooden boat weaves through the hundreds of islands that surround Stockholm. Some are no more than a clump of trees seemingly floating in the water, while others are brightened by picturebook little summer houses each with its own small boathouse at the water's edge. Many beautiful green lakes are traversed as the boat cuts across country, frequently majestic white swans glide amongst the low reeds that line the shore. But the most exciting part of this trip is passing through the narrow rivers and canals where trees brush the sides of the boat, toy-like gingerbread houses nestle in green lawns, beautiful blond children wave merrily from the shore, boys on bikes race beside the boat, handsome youngsters shout hello from passing sailboats and old men pause in their fishing as the boat passes. This canal trip is rather like a house party as the passengers become friends while sharing the fun of this nostalgic canal adventure.

DESTINATION VIII GOTHENBURG Hotel Ekoxen

The HOTEL EKOXEN us a very pleasant small hotel with a light, cheerful ambiance, conveniently located within walking diatance of much of Gothenburg's sightseeing. If you arrive by boat, the hotel is a short taxi ride from the pier. If you arrive by train, the station is only two blocks away.

GOTHENBURG, the second largest city in Sweden, cannot rival Stockholm for charm. However, it is an interesting old city with a bustling port where ships arrive from all over the world. There are several interesting things to do here. One of the most interesting is a boat excursion which explores the canals and the giant harbor. Shopping is good, with nice shops located along a series of interconnecting pedestrian-only streets. If you like markets, you might want to get up early to see one of the largest fish auctions in Scandinavia - a colorful confusion of wholesalers auctioning off every kind of fish imaginable. If you enjoy churches, be sure to visit the ORGRYTE CHURCH, dating from the 13th century, with its beautiful ceiling paintings. If the weather is pleasant, you might want to visit the greenhouse (called the PALMHUSET) located across the road from the train station.

Hotel Ekoxen
Gothenburg

DESTINATION IX COPENHAGEN The Plaza Hotel

It is a pleasant journey from Gothenburg to Copenhagen. The train and ferry are coordinated so that you do not have to worry about any connections. The train goes to Helsingborg and boards the ferry for the 20-minute ride across the channel to Denmark where, upon arrival, the train rolls off the ferry and continues on to Copenhagen.

In summer, there are five departures a day between Gothenburg and Copenhagen. The following is a convenient possible choice:

12:30 pm leave Gothenburg by train
5:05 pm arrive Copenhagen

Upon arrival in COPENHAGEN you will find THE PLAZA HOTEL directly across from train station, a wonderful location and an ideal base for your sightseeing. Originally referred to as the Hotel Terminus, The Plaza Hotel was built at the command of King Frederik VIII of Denmark to coincide with the 1911 opening of the new Central Station. Although the hotel was not completed until 1914, since its opening it has set for itself a high standard of excellence and prides itself on personalized service.

The Plaza Hotel
Copenhagen

A delight for the young and old, Copenhagen has many aspects to its character. Founded in the year 1167, the city has enjoyed regal stature as home to the Danish kings and queens since 1417 and by contrast is internationally known for sheltering within its boundaries one of the world's largest amusement parks whose fireworks regularly add magic to the summer night sky. A statue of a little mermaid stands watch over the entrance to one of the world's busiest harbors. Monuments, towers, churches, a castle and palaces tell stories of a past steeped in history. Theaters, concert halls, galleries, nightclubs, hotels, restaurants and shops found along old winding streets, facing onto open squares, or in restored old buildings provide a contemporary lifestyle and 24-hour pace for this international city.

Copenhagen is a city to be explored and is intimate enough in scale to delight the pedestrian. Every square, cobblestoned street and grand boulevard exposes new aspects and dimensions to the image of the city. Every Sunday in summer English-speaking guides conduct a two-hour walking tour of the city. Coach tours are, of course, also available and often include a visit to a brewery or sights on the city's outskirts. In warm summer months, a tour of Copenhagen's streets is enhanced by a trip through its transecting canals. (Details and information on all tours, including private ones, may be obtained through the Danish Tourist Office, adjacent to Tivoli Gardens: H.C. Andersens Blvd 22, DK-1553 Copenhagen V, tel: (01) 11 14 15.) Whether you venture out with a guide or on your own, there are certain attractions that are a "must" for your itinerary.

From May through September TIVOLI GARDENS is one of Copenhagen's most popular destinations. Its own fairytale world at the heart Copenhagen, Tivoli is a magical complex of garden, amusement park and cultural center. There are garden cafes, restaurants and beer gardens to enjoy while ballet, mime, concerts and fireworks provide an endless variety of entertainment. For the children and children-at-heart the amusement park has a number of wonderful rides. Open day and night, the glitter and sparkle of Tivoli is infectious and sounds of laughter from the park float across the city.

Abounding in character, NYHAVN, although translated to mean New Harbor, is the old port of Copenhagen. Tall narrow buildings of varying salt-water weathered facades with tile and slate roofs huddle together to line the narrow canal passageways. Although cafe tables cluster on the narrow walkway bordering the waterfront and charming restaurants, accommodations and antique shops are found in weathered buildings that were once old sailor haunts, the waterways are still home for all sorts of vessels from rugged tugboats to majestic schooners with their tall, willowy masts. Myhavn is a delightful district to explore.

Another fascinating area is the old university section, the LATIN QUARTER, which gravitates around the popular, airy square, Graabroedretorv. Winding cobbled streets are a mecca for sidewalk cafes and charming restaurants. This is a district that comes to life and is particularly captivating on warm sunny days.

The history of Copenhagen can be seen in its palaces, towers and churches. ROSENBORG CASTLE is a Renaissance castle built by Christian IV, today housing the crown jewels and private belongings of the Danish royalty. It is open daily from May to October. AMALIENBORG PALACE has been the royal residence since 1794 and although it is not open to the public, the changing of the guard takes place in full pomp and circumstance in the palace square when the Queen is in residence. You can participate in the fanfare by following the parade of guards from their barracks in front of Rosenborg Castle (11:30 am) to the square in front of the palace. The actual changing of the guard takes place around noon.

Copenhagen boasts a wide variety of museums to investigate. The NATIONAL MUSEUM displays artifacts primarily from the Bronze and Viking Ages and ethnographical collections. The ROYAL MUSEUM OF FINE ARTS has Danish paintings and sculptures and European paintings on exhibit. The TOY MUSEUM, the THEATER HISTORY MUSEUM and the ROYAL STABLES hold special appeal for children. The ROYAL ARSENAL MUSEUM houses an international collection of arms and uniforms.

Much of the architecture in Copenhagen was detailed to enhance the beauty of the city. Towers and spires of some very distinguished churches serve to provide a unique skyline. A fine example of a building from the 1600s is HOLMEN'S CHURCH and from the 1700s OUR SAVIOR'S CHURCH.

STROGET is Copenhagen's principal shopping street. Closed to traffic, this winding, cobbled street is lined by an assortment of shops and galleries, affording the best of Danish design: porcelain, silver, glass, furniture and much more. This is a district of interest to the non-shopper as well, as streets broaden out to accommodate a colorful array of peddlers and musicians plus flower, fruit and ice-cream stalls.

The loveliest and most romantic stroll in Copenhagen is along the Langeliniepavillonen and out to the statue of the LITTLE MERMAID. This enchanting maiden beckons ships from all over the world, as well as guarding the entrance to the city's harbor. This small bronze sculpture, designed by Edvard Eriksen in 1913, has captured the hearts of tourists from around the world and has become a symbol of Copenhagen.

Copenhagen is a delightful city and a perfect conclusion to any holiday. If time allows, try to extend your stay in Denmark by joining one of the countryside itineraries: "Viking Trails of Denmark", "Dramatic Castles of Sealand", or "The Fairytale Island of Funen".

The Little Mermaid
Copenhagen

Note: Reservations for the boats and trains described in this itinerary, "Highlights of Scandinavia by Train & Boat", can be made through your travel agent or booked directly through the following companies:

SCANWORLD (booking agent for Gota Canal trips)
12444 Ventura Blvd.
Studio City, CA 91604
(818) 506-4114

SILJA LINE (ferry between Sweden and Finland)
c/o Bergen Line
505 Fifth Avenue
New York, NY 10017
(212) 986-2711

VIKING LINE (ferry between Sweden and Finland)
c/o Scantours
1535 6th Street, Suite 209
Santa Monica, CA 90401
(213) 451-0911

FRENCH NATIONAL RAILROADS (trains throughout Scandinavia)
610 Fifth Avenue
New York, NY 10020
(212) 582-4813

GERMAN FEDERAL RAILROAD (trains throughout Scandinavia)
747 Third Avenue
New York, NY 10017
(212) 308-3100

Scenic Journey from Stockholm

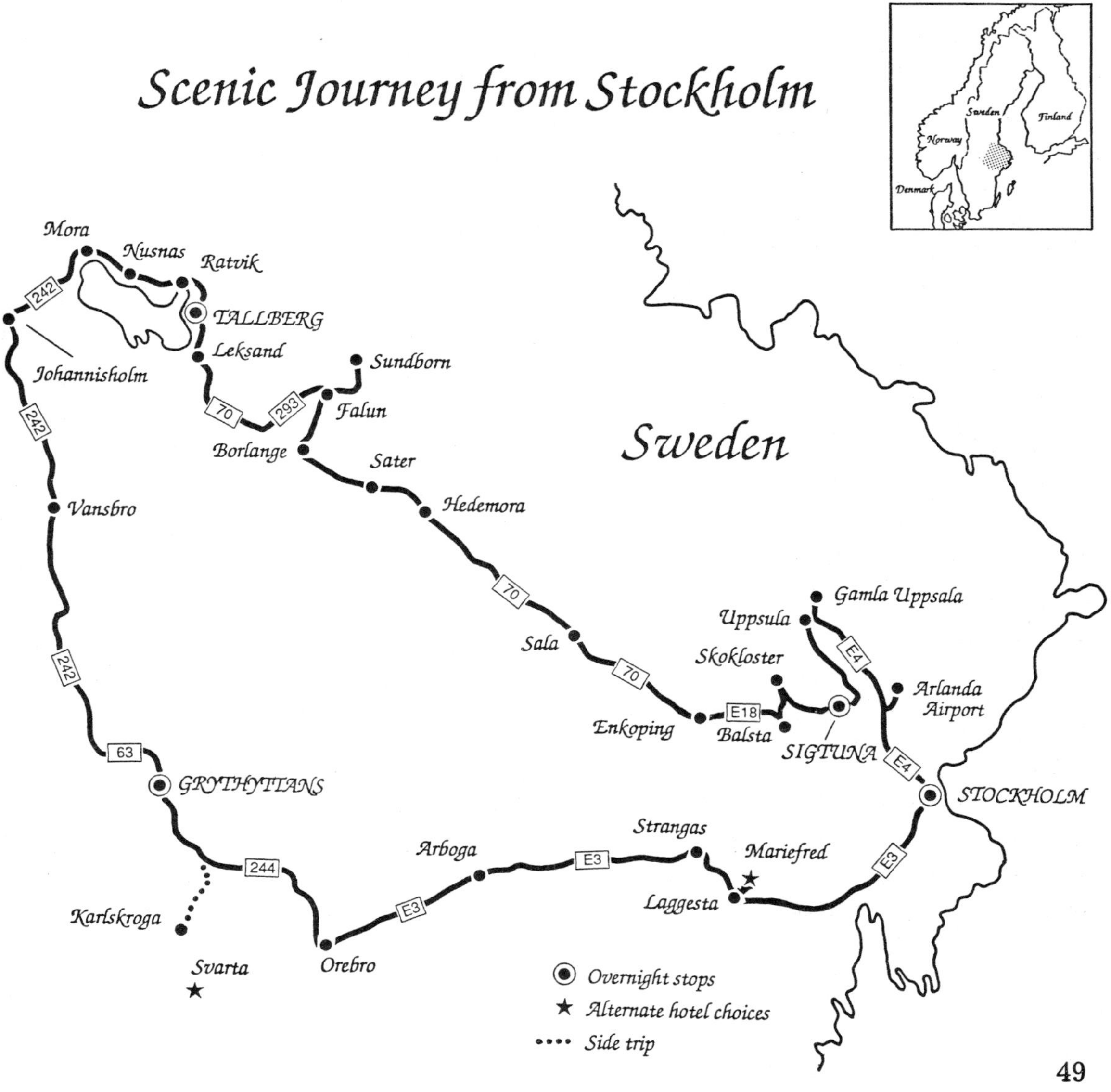

Sweden
Norway
Finland
Denmark

Sweden

Mora
Nusnas
Ratvik
TALLBERG
Leksand
Sundborn
Johannisholm
Falun
Borlange
Sater
Hedemora
Vansbro
Sala
Gamla Uppsala
Uppsula
Skokloster
Arlanda Airport
Enkoping
Balsta
SIGTUNA
STOCKHOLM
GRYTHYTTANS
Strangas
Arboga
Mariefred
Laggesta
Karlskroga
Svarta
Orebro

242
242
242
70
293
70
70
E18
E4
E4
63
244
E3
E3
E3

Overnight stops
Alternate hotel choices
Side trip

Scenic Journey from Stockholm

Stockholm is one of Europe's most entrancing cities. Using Stockholm as a base, you can capture the flavor of Sweden's rural beauty by taking wonderful daytrips into the countryside. But, if you prefer to take your sightseeing at a leisurely pace and stay each night in a village hotel, rather than rushing back to the city, this itinerary is perfect for you. With this short itinerary you meander through some of Sweden's most beautiful scenery and visit some of her most charming towns - all within an easy drive of Stockholm. If you have sufficient time, this itinerary makes a perfect introduction to "Splendors of Southern Sweden", the itinerary which immediately follows this one.

Mariefred

ORIGINATING CITY STOCKHOLM

STOCKHOLM is built on a series of islands. The medieval part of town (called GAMLA STAN) is situated on its own little island connected by a causeway to the center of the "New Stockholm". Gamla Stan is bursting with charm and as you walk around you are surrounded by the spirit of yesteryear. Allow plenty of time to do justice to the many sights of Stockholm before sampling the countryside. There are many historical places to visit and fascinating boat trips to take. Suggestions on what to see and do are covered in detail beginning on page 33.

DESTINATION I SIGTUNA Stadshotellet

The drive today is short, the first night's destination purposely chosen close to Stockholm to allow you ample time to enjoy the interesting sights en route. Leave Stockholm by the well marked freeway E4 heading north: signs are posted for Arlanda Airport which you pass about half an hour after leaving the city. Follow the freeway for the 70-kilometer drive to the university town of UPPSALA, but do not go into the city center: stay on the E4 as it skirts the edge of the town, following signs for GAMLA UPPSALA (Old Uppsala). Here, in an open field, you will find Viking burial mounds dating from the 6th century. Nearby is a small 12th-century church, very important in medieval times when Swedish kings were crowned here. Across from the church is DISAGARDEN, an open-air museum where old houses collected from the surrounding area have been brought. You must visit the quaint ODINSBORG TAVERN, a delightful old hostelry and tea room where it is great fun to enjoy a snack and drink mead, like the Vikings used to do - out of silver-tipped ox horns.

After visiting the old town, drive south into the heart of the new - which isn't really new at all, for UPPSALA is a delightful medieval town. Park your car and with map in hand set out to explore. Stroll along the Fyrisa River as it meanders through the center of town, look for the twin spires of the UPPSALA CATHEDRAL, the largest in Scandinavia. When you spot the spires, leave the river and take the short uphill walk to the 15th-century cathedral. The magnificent Gothic interior with its beautiful, intricately designed vaulted ceiling is a delight, and there are many tombs, several with excellent sculptures. The pulpit is a splendid example of baroque art. Leaving the cathedral, it is only a short walk to the UPPSALA UNIVERSITY LIBRARY, where there are most interesting displays of beautiful old manuscripts and books: with over two million books, this is Sweden's largest library. From the university, walk across the park to see the 16th-century UPPSALA CASTLE with its dungeons and Coronation Hall. The castle is open to visitors in the summer.

Stadshotellet
Sigtuna

After visiting Uppsala, return south on the road that leads you through ALSIKE to SIGTUNA, about a 30-kilometer drive. This small village, one of the oldest in Sweden, oozes with charm. It is like a stage setting, with colorful shops and houses lining each side of the pedestrian main street. In the center of town, a park slopes down to the lake where in summer hundreds of sailboats dot the water. Basically, Sigtuna is a town for shopping and soaking in the olde-worlde atmosphere, but, if you want to sightsee, there are several places of interest: the colorful 18th-century TOWN HALL is the smallest in Sweden; the 13th-century ST MARY'S MONASTERY has some nice wall paintings; the LUNDSTROMSKE (an attractive old burgher's home) has some handsome antique furnishings and the ruins of ST PER'S (Sweden's oldest cathedral) has great historical interest.

Your hotel for tonight, the STADSHOTELLET, is located on the main street in town, just beyond the shopping section. This hotel was built at the beginning of the 20th century and is rather plain, without the charm of the colorful older buildings on the street. However, it is the best hotel in town and has a good restaurant. The bedrooms on the upper floors facing the lake have especially attractive views so be sure to request one of these.

DESTINATION II TALLBERG Akerblads Hotel

After leaving Sigtuna, your first stop is SKOKLOSTER CASTLE, a short 16-kilometer drive to the northwest. The road makes a loop around the lake before reaching the 17th-century castle. This is not a fortress-style castle with massive fortifications, but rather a large white four-story structure punctuated with many windows and enhanced by octagonal towers on each corner. The interior is in excellent condition, with beautiful paintings on the walls. Of special interest is the weapons collection. Car buffs will want to pay a visit to the Motor Museum in the grounds which houses Sweden's largest vintage car collection.

From Skokloster Castle, head south to the E18 and then west, following signs for ENKOPING. Take the bypass circling north around Enkoping and continue northwest on the 70, following signs for SALA, a 14th-century silver town. About 40 kilometers beyond Sala, you come to HEDEMORA, one of the most charming towns en route. Stop to see the main square whose interesting old buildings include a lovely old town hall, an 18th-century red-timbered pharmacy, the old theater and the 15th-century church. Another 11-kilometer drive brings you to SATER, famous for the making of tile stoves. When you reach BORLANGE turn north on the 60 toward FALUN where copper has been mined for over 1,000 years. If time permits, you can take a guided tour of one of the mines.

From Falun, turn east on highway 80 for about 9 kilometers to KORSNAS where you take a small road north to SUNDBORN. This is where Sweden's beloved artist Carl Larsson lived in his little house beside the lake with his beautiful wife, Karin, and their six children. Carl Larsson spent his life painting his family and his home, which is now open as a small museum. Those of you who are familiar with Larsson's work will treasure the tour which takes you through the house where you will recognize every nook and corner from his whimsical paintings, filled with fun and laughter and poignancy.

Retrace your steps to Falun and take the 293 to the intersection of 70 and then turn right driving northwest to LEKSAND. Soon after Leksand, take a road to the left which skirts the eastern shore of the lake and heads north to TALLBERG.

There are several excellent choices for accommodation in Tallberg, one of the nicest being the AKERBLADS HOTEL, located near the center of town. This hotel is brimming with charm, with many tastefully displayed country antiques giving a cozy, welcoming atmosphere. The bedrooms are all pleasant, but the suites are not expensive and are especially inviting - large, airy and nicely decorated with antiques. The Akerblads' dining room is not only extremely attractive, but serves exceptionally fine food.

Akerblads Hotel
Tallberg

Tallberg is located in the province of Sweden called DALARNA which, for the Swedes as well as tourists, is an exceptionally popular destination for a holiday. Dalarna is a beautiful area of Sweden and the town of Tallberg typifies the best of what Dalarna has to offer. Here you will see almost all of the wood-frame farmhouses painted with the same colors. Many of the farms are very old, but even the new conform to the same style of architecture and are painted red with white trim. There is a very special appeal to this part of Sweden: Lake Siljan, lovely forests, continuity of architecture, pretty farms, and, above all, wonderfully friendly people make this a delightful area to visit.

DESTINATION III GRYTHYTTAN Grythyttans Gastgivaregard

You may want to linger in Tallberg to enjoy long walks through the peaceful countryside and take one of the boat rides on Lake Siljan. When you do leave, drive directly north along the lake to RATVIK where, beside the lake, there is a very old, very lovely little church perched above the water's edge. A fascinating aspect of the church is the cluster of 90 tiny wooden huts built near the lake. These were constructed to encourage the congregation to attend church - no matter what the weather. Many of the church members would arrive either by horse or by boat. If a storm came, and those who came to church could not make it home again the same day, the huts offered shelter for them (and their horses).

From Ratvik continue north, following the small road that traces the eastern edge of the lake. In approximately 18 kilometers you arrive at the small town of NUSNAS, the center of the world-famous, brightly painted, gaily decorated, little wooden horses which have become so popular that they have become a symbol of Sweden. These sturdy little horses, painted either red or blue, are carved in several small factories in Nusnas. There are signs directing you to the small workshops, each of which has a store where you can buy not only the horses, but also many other handmade wooden souvenirs.

Take the 70 out of Nusnas, following signs to MORA, located at the northern tip of the lake. Stop in Mora to visit the ZORN MUSEUM. Anders Zorn (1860-1920), one of Sweden's most famous painters, lived and painted here. His turn-of-the-century home and a museum (located on the same property) are open to the public and the museum contains many fine examples of his and his contemporaries' paintings.

From Mora head southwest along the 234. At JOHANNISHOLM the road divides, but stay on the 234 which heads directly south. The next part of your journey is not filled with sightseeing, but brimming with beauty. For about two hours you drive through a beautiful area of green forests, many lakes and rushing rivers.

When you reach the junction of the 234 and the 63, turn left (east). In about 17 kilometers when you come to the 244, head south. In just minutes you see a turn to the right to the small village of GRYTHYTTAN. Driving into town, you see your hotel, the GRYTHYTTANS GASTGIVAREGARD. This is a very special establishment, one of the most beautifully managed small hotels in Sweden. The lounges and dining rooms are filled with superb antiques, and the guestrooms (although quite small) are color-coordinated with a sophisticated touch. The food is expensive but sensational. The Grythyttans Gastgivaregard has gradually incorporated the entire town (except the village church) into the hotel. Some of the small houses have been converted into guest rooms while others now sport pretty little shops.

Grythyttans Gastgivaregard
Grythyttan

While in Grythyttan, if you are an admirer of the great industrialist and philanthropist Alfred Nobel, ask directions at the hotel for the back road which heads directly south to KARLSKOGA where Nobel lived and worked. His home with its library, study and laboratory still intact are open every afternoon during the summer.

When you leave Grythyttan return to the 244 and drive southeast until you come to the 60 where you turn south toward OREBRO. Just before you reach Orebro, turn east on the E3. (At the town of ARBOGA the highway splits and both branches continue into Stockholm - be sure to stay on the E3.)

There is only one sightseeing excursion suggested for today, but it is so very special that it deserves your entire attention. As you drive along the E3 about 18 kilometers beyond the town of STRANGNAS, watch for LAGGESTA where you turn to the left on the road marked to MARIEFRED. After the turnoff, it is only a few minutes further to Mariefred, which is not only one of Sweden's most picturesque little towns, but also the site of one of Sweden's most beautiful castles. Mariefred, located on the shore of Lake Malar, dates back to the 15th century and maintains its wonderful olde-worlde ambiance. It still has many colorful wooden houses, a beautiful church whose spire pokes up above the village, an old wooden town hall on the market square and many narrow little lanes. Located next to the harbor where the ferry arrives from Stockholm is the oldest hotel in Sweden, the GRIPSHOLMS VARDSHUS, an excellent choice for lunch or a snack. Across a tiny bay from the hotel you can see GRIPSHOLMS CASTLE: definitely make time to include this castle in your sightseeing since it is just super. The setting is wonderful, with the massive 16th-century castle completely dominating a tiny island connected to the mainland by a drawbridge. Crossing the drawbridge, you enter into a large central courtyard before walking up some steps into the castle which boasts the world's largest collection of portraits.

From Mariefred, return to highway E3 for an easy drive into Stockholm where you can settle in for some more sightseeing, join one of our other itineraries or take a train, ship or airplane to your next destination.

Splendors of Southern Sweden

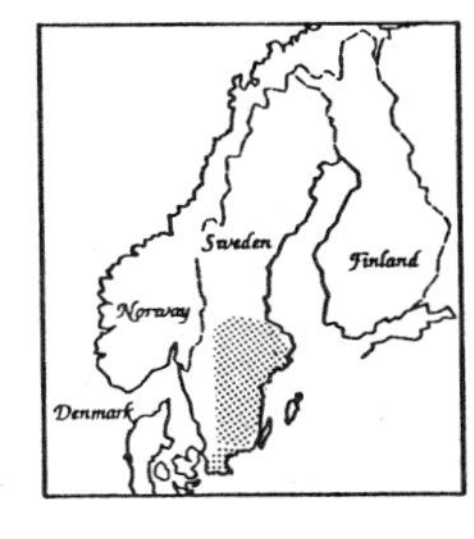

Splendors of Southern Sweden

Sweden offers some of the most delightful sightseeing and beautiful scenery in all of Europe, yet far too many tourists visit only Stockholm - what a shame. Allow time to meander into the countryside, discover colorful villages, lovely lakes, beautiful farms, spectacular castles, glorious beaches and quaint windmills, and - best of all - meet the Swedes whose warmth and graciousness make a holiday memorable. This itinerary begins in Stockholm and makes a loop through southern Sweden - returning to Stockholm. However, if you are planning to take the ferry to Denmark, you can take the first part of this itinerary to Helsingborg or Malmo. Or, vice versa, you can take the ferry from Denmark and choose one of the legs of the loop to make your way to Stockholm. If you have sufficient time, combine this itinerary with "Scenic Journey from Stockholm" which includes sightseeing to the north of Stockholm.

Kalmar Castle

ORIGINATING CITY STOCKHOLM

STOCKHOLM makes an ideal starting point for any Swedish itinerary because it is so conveniently accessible by plane, ship or train. There are many excellent choices of hotels in Stockholm: the hotel section includes several in the charming old section called "GAMLA STAN" where you are immersed in the atmosphere of bygone days. There are many wonderful sights to see and excursions to take while in Stockholm and our sightseeing suggestions for this beautiful city begin on page 33.

DESTINATION I SVARTA Svarta Herrgard

When you are ready to begin your excursion, drive north from Stockholm along the E4 freeway. The Stockholm Arlanda Airport is along this same route, so you can follow the airport signs which are well posted. Just before you come to the airport take the 263 MARSTA turnoff to SIGTUNA, about a 15-minute drive from the freeway.

Sigtuna was once the capital of Sweden, but now this tiny town is mostly visited for its picture-perfect main street lined with charming olde-worlde houses and shops. Stop in one of the colorful pastry shops for a snack and browse through the many quaint gift stores. If you want to do some sightseeing, visit the 13th-century ST MARY'S CHURCH and the ruins of ST PER'S, Sweden's oldest cathedral.

From Sigtuna, follow the 263 south and connect with the E18 heading west to ENKOPING. Take the bypass which circles to the north of Enkoping and on to the small city of VASTERAS. From Vasteras, stay on the E18 all the way to KARLSKOGA where, during the summer season, ALFRED NOBEL'S HOME is open to the public in the afternoons. It is interesting to see the residence of this brilliant man known worldwide for the Nobel prizes which honor some of the great benefactors to humanity. The prizes are given each year to compensate the world for the devastation wrought by his invention - dynamite.

From Karlskoga, take the 205 south to DEGERFORS, from where it is only a 15-kilometer drive to SVARTA.

Svarta Herrgard
Svarta

As you drive through Svarta you cannot miss the SVARTA HERRGARD - it is a lovely old manor, easily seen on the left-hand side of the road. Drive through the front gates and into the inner courtyard formed by the main inn flanked by two smaller annexes on either side. From the front, the hotel is quite pleasing, but its main attribute cannot be appreciated until you enter the hotel, walk through to the rear and see the lawn stretching out to an idyllic, tree-lined lake. The hotel has its own little pier and strategically placed lounges where you can rest and enjoy the glorious scenery. Inside, the hotel is very pleasant, with many antiques accenting the somewhat formal mood. One of the best features are the lovely bedrooms with views of the lake - when making reservations, request one of these.

DESTINATION II GRANNA Vastana Slott

Leaving Svarta, take the 205 south to ASKERSUND and then the 50 south to MOTALA. The road follows the eastern shore of Sweden's second largest lake, Lake Vattern, which is very deep and very clear - you can see the sandy bottom at depths of over 20 feet. One of the reasons the water is so clear is that it is partially fed by springs. The lake is also famous for a very special Vattern salmon - a delicious fish and a great delicacy served at many of the restaurants and hotels in the area. Be sure to try it.

From Motala it is only about 16 kilometers to VADSTENA, your first sightseeing stop of the day. Plan to have lunch here and spend several hours enjoying this delightful lakeside village. Vadstena has carefully nurtured its olde-worlde ambiance - this is truly a picture-postcard village. But it isn't only for its charm that Vadstena is so enticing: there are several places of interest to visit. Park in the square and walk to Birgitta's abbey. Birgitta was of noble birth and the mother of eight children when God appeared to her in a vision. After her religious experience she left her family and founded her own religious order, building the VADSTENA ABBEY. Part of the abbey is now an inn (KLOSTERS GUESTHOUSE), but of principal interest is the strikingly powerful, yet simple in design, Gothic Abbey Church, designed by Birgitta.

After visiting the abbey walk along the parklike promenade to see VADSTENA CASTLE, an impressive 16th-century fortress surrounded by a moat crossed over by a drawbridge. Most of the castle is closed, but one wing houses a small art museum. Wind your way through the narrow little streets back to the main square, perhaps browsing through the shops displaying the famous Vadstena handmade lace.

From Vadstena it is about an hour's drive (depending upon traffic) to GRANNA. Your road, the 50, joins the E4 and becomes a freeway, making the drive faster. Take the turnoff for Granna and stop to see this idyllic 17th-century village built on an incline above Lake Vattern. The town still maintains its quaint olde-worlde charm and, amazingly, many of its old wooden buildings are still intact.

Vastana Slott
Granna

After a quick trip to see Granna, do not return to the freeway but take the side road to VASTANA. The road parallels the highway and passes through ROTTLE, a picturesque cluster of colorful old houses, then sweeps under the freeway and up the hill, ending at your hotel for tonight, the VASTANA SLOTT.

This is a very special hotel with only nine rooms, but large on charm and personalized service. The owner, Rolf von Otter, was born here. It is still his home, but he and his beautiful wife open it to guests during the summer: you really feel like a guest in a private home while staying here. The furnishings reflect the grandeur of the past, with fabulous antiques that have been in the family for many generations. Also, ask Rolf von Otter to show you old pictures of the castle - it is fascinating to see the structural changes over the years. Breakfast is the only meal served but this is no problem as there are restaurants close at hand. There is a restaurant with an especially good view across the lake at GYLLENE UTTERN, a nearby hotel built by Rolf von Otter's family in 1932.

DESTINATION III VITTARYD Toftaholm Manor House

When you leave Vastana Slott return to the E4 and follow signs for JONKOPING, 35 kilometers away at the southern tip of Lake Vattern. Jonkoping is a busy commercial city which is host to many fairs and exhibitions. Its main claim to fame is that safety matches were invented here by the Lundstrom brothers in 1845. The original MATCH FACTORY, a picturesque blue clapboard building, has been converted to a museum showing the history of fire and the progression to today's matches. The museum is located near the lake at Vastra Storgatan 18A, and is open Monday through Saturday.

After visiting the match museum return to the E4 and continue south for the 60-kilometer drive to VARNAMO. This road passes through some lovely pine forests and several small towns. As you leave Varnamo the road passes by LAKE VIDOSTERN and through the town of TANGO - watch carefully for your hotel, TOFTAHOLM MANOR HOUSE, because, although the address shows Vittaryd, that is only the mailing address: the hotel itself is not in town, but in the countryside. It is not difficult to find: just keep watching on the right for the entrance. A small lane leads to the hotel where you park in a courtyard framed by the main manor house flanked by two smaller annexes. This inn is owned by Jan and Lisbeth Boethius, a very gracious, very professional young couple who recently bought this idyllic manor which had become dilapidated and transformed it into a charming, comfortable inn. There is a wonderful, homey atmosphere and the decor is comfy and inviting. Antiques adorn the light and airy rooms. The setting is fabulous - right on the lake with a lawn stretching out to the edge of the water where a few colorful rowboats are tied up, tantalizingly available for a lazy excursion. Just a short stroll from the inn a tiny bridge leads across to a forested little island.

If you like the out-of-doors, this is a perfect place to break your journey. Jan Boethius can show you wonderful walks through a parklike forest very close to the hotel. Or, if you prefer rowing, small boats are available and you can spend the day exploring the lake.

Toftaholm Manor House
Vittaryd

When you leave Toftaholm Manor House, return to the E4 and drive south to MARKARYD. If you are going on to Copenhagen, continue on the E4 which goes straight to HELSINGBORG where frequent ferries cross the narrow channel to Denmark. If you are completing the loop of Southern Sweden, turn left at Markaryd following the 117 for the 40-kilometer drive to HASSLEHOLM, then take the 21 east to KRISTIANSTAD where you pick up the E66 (sometimes called the 15) and continue east for about 10 kilometers to FJALKINGE. When you reach Fjalkinge, watch carefully for a sign for a road to the left which winds through the countryside for a few kilometers to the BACKASKOG SLOTT.

Backaskog Slott
Fjalkinge

When you arrive at Backaskog Slott, go to the ticket agent's booth near the gate and tell him you are a guest at the hotel: he will let you drive into the central courtyard where you park your car and then register with the proprietor Gerhard Marz. The castle is surrounded by lovely gardens and its own small forest where there are a few cottages which can be rented and several rather drab motel-like annexes. The most charming accommodation is in the main castle which has a small selection of rooms. All are attractively decorated although most do not have private bathrooms. There is a bridal suite which is expensive, spacious and most inviting. Since you will be staying here for at least a couple of nights while you explore the chateau country, the suite would be most comfortable. It has its own cozy entry hall, a nicely decorated living room and a lovely bedroom with windows overlooking the garden.

After getting settled, ask Gerhard Marz to give you a tour of his interesting castle. In the 13th century it was a monastery, established by wily monks on a small stream connecting two lakes. The stream ran through the central courtyard, so the monks could fish and get water without ever leaving their sanctuary. Later the monastery was taken over by the king and converted to a castle. The building is in excellent condition with four wings, joined at the corners by small towers, forming a central courtyard. The old stables now house the cafeteria whose rustic decor reflects its past. One wing of the castle is a museum with an excellent display of antique furniture; another wing is used for guestrooms, while a tiny chapel is tucked into a third wing.

Throughout Sweden there are many beautiful castles, but the greatest abundance of them are in the south where every few miles you discover another fairytale chateau. Although most of these are privately owned, many are open to the public and even those which are not, are fun to glimpse from the road. Backaskog Slott, a tourist attraction as well as your hotel, makes an excellent base from which to explore Sweden's Chateau Country. On the next page is a map followed by a suggested itinerary to help you plan your excursion into this very special part of Sweden.

The Chateau Country of Southern Sweden

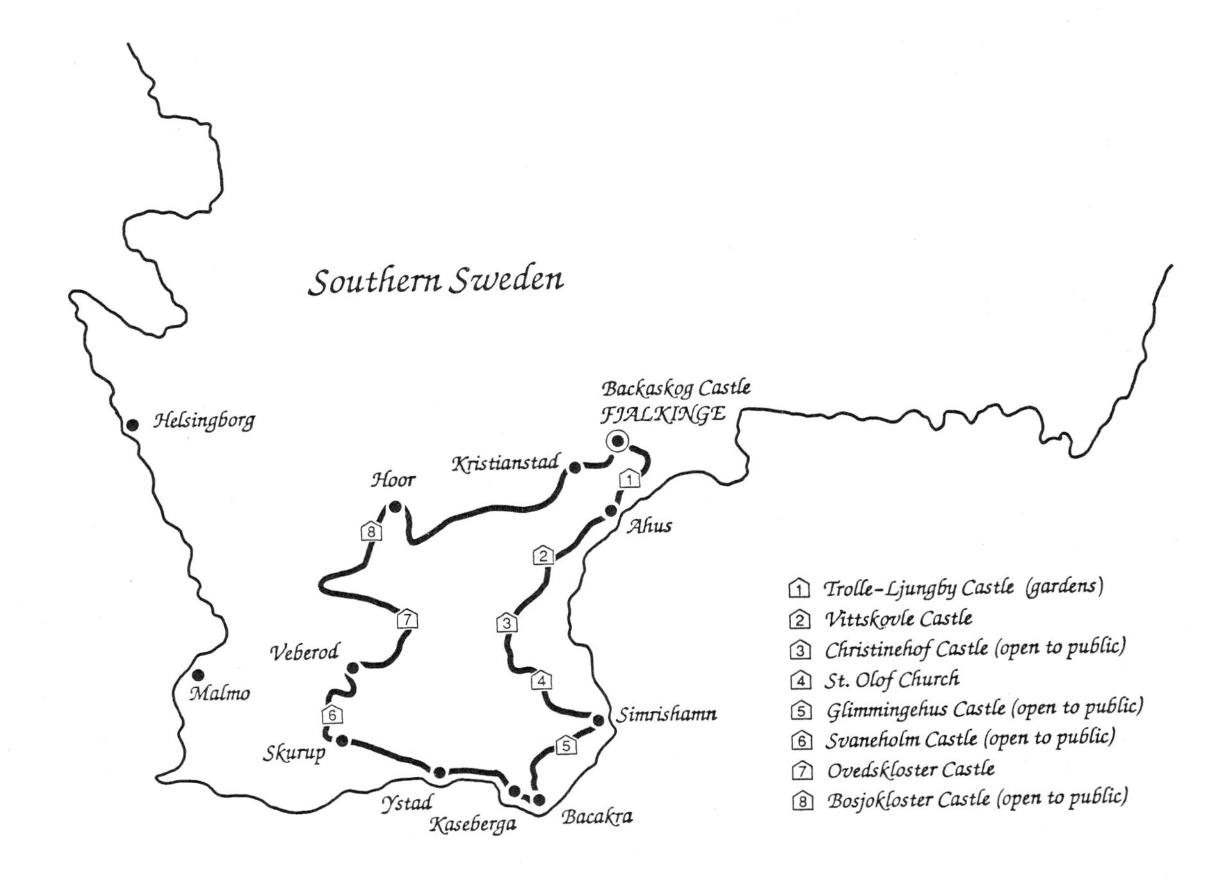

The Chateau Country

This excursion encompasses some of the loveliest countryside in all of Sweden: a land of rolling hills, small forests, enormous old farmhouses, and best of all - a land dotted with picturesque chateaux. To visit this area any time of year is a delight, but in May the farms are surrounded by fields of dazzling mustard-yellow flowers - a very special sight you will always remember.

As you read through this excursion you will notice that many of the roads are described rather vaguely without a road number. This is because these little back roads are too small to be labeled. So, before starting, purchase as detailed a map as possible showing some of the castles you will see. Even with a good map you may get lost, but this is not a problem as distances are so short that you will soon find yourself on a marked road and will quickly be able to establish where you are. Getting lost is half the fun because the countryside is so lovely. Dawdling along the way at a favorite castle or charming little chapel, you might not be able to include all the castles. Not to worry when the evening grows late: abandon further sightseeing and navigate a direct route to Backaskog, your own castle for the night.

To begin your excursion, return to the E66 and turn left (east) for just a few minutes until you see signs to the right heading south to TROLLE-LJUNGBY CASTLE. This road weaves through the countryside the short distance to the castle just before the town of VANNEBERGA. The castle is surrounded by a small moat and, although it is a private residence, the gardens are open to the public in summer on Wednesdays and Saturdays.

Continue southwest toward RINKABY and take the 118 south to the port of AHUS. Visit the beautiful church in the center of town before taking a small back road heading southwest toward DEGEBERGA. Just before you reach the town you arrive at VITTSKOVLE CASTLE, a privately owned 16th-century castle surrounded by a large moat and park.

From Vittskovle Castle a road heads directly south and intersects the 20. Turn left (southeast) on the 20 and continue to BROSARP. From here a small back road weaves through the countryside to CHRISTINEHOF CASTLE. This 18th-century chateau-style castle, owned by Count Carl Piper, still retains much of its original furnishings and is open to the public in the summer from 11:00 am to 8:00 pm. A restaurant serves snacks and drinks.

From Christinehof Castle, drive southeast, rejoin the 20 and head south to FAGELTOFTA where you can see, but not visit, the 18th-century KRONOVALL CASTLE.

Stop in ST OLOF to see its especially lovely old church. Continue directly east until you intersect the 10 and head south following signs for SIMRISHAMN. On the outskirts Simrishamn does not appear very interesting, but when you drive to the heart of the old section which centers around the harbor you find a charming medieval town with many half-timbered buildings. If you are ready for lunch, a good choice is the HOTEL KOCHSKA GARDEN, an old coaching inn with a beautiful black-and-white-timbered facade. Before leaving town, be sure to visit the 12th-century ST NICHOLAI CHURCH where you see a fascinating display of model ships hung from the ceiling.

From Simrishamn, take the 12 west to TOMMARP where a small road directs you south to GLIMMINGEHUS CASTLE. Although unfurnished, this 15th-century moated castle is fascinating. Cross the bridge and explore this small stone building with its stepped gabled tile roof then climb the narrow staircase to enjoy the serene views of the countryside framed by small windows.

From Glimmingehus take the small road south to HOBY, visit the old church and then go southwest on the 10. Just before you reach LODERUP, turn south and join the coastal road called Kasebergaasen. At the point where you come to Kasebergaasen, you see signs for BACAKRA, Dag Hammarskjold's farm where he would have retired had it not been for his untimely death in a plane crash. A small lane leads to his home which is open as a museum during the summer from 1:00 pm to 5:00 pm. The home is intimate and very interesting, with lots of souvenirs that Hammarskjold collected as he travelled the world. It is set amongst fields which sweep out to the headlands.

After visiting Hammarskjold's farm, continue west along the Kasebergaasen for a very short distance until you come to a small road that leads to KASEBERGA. In just a few minutes you come to the sea and a cluster of fish factories along the wharf where eels are smoked and processed. Leave your car in the parking area and follow the small path which climbs the bluff to the meadow above the sea. Here in a beautiful setting are 57 giant stones marking the perimeter of a Viking ship, probably the grave of some great Viking chief. Except for the stones, there is not much to see. However, the setting is so untouched by commercialism and the view so lovely this interlude is definitely worth a stop.

After seeing Kaseberga (and perhaps poking your head in to watch the fish being smoked in one of the little warehouses), continue along the coastal road toward YSTAD, a small city with many medieval buildings. Stroll through the old section of town. Of special interest is the GRAY FRIARS' MONASTERY, a 13th-century monastery almost as well preserved as the one you saw in Vadstena.

Leaving Ystad, take the E14 northwest out of town. Very shortly after leaving town you pass MARSVINSCHOLM CASTLE, a lovely 17th-century moated castle which you can view only from the road since it is not open to the public.

Continue west on the E4 until you see signs for SVANEHOLM CASTLE (located about 23 kilometers west of Ystad, near the town of SKURUP). Svaneholm, dating from the 16th century, was once a fortress. Today the castle is owned by the Co-operative Society of Svaneholm and the Archeological Society who open it to the public every day except Monday during the summer season.

From Svaneholm, follow the small road north past the privately owned

HACKEBERGA CASTLE idyllically set on its own little island in the lake. From Hackeberga Castle a small road leads you east to the 13 north to VEBEROD. At Veberod turn west for a few kilometers to a road heading north toward OVED and OVEDSKLOSTER CASTLE. This beautiful castle was built in the 18th century but dates back to the 12th century when a monastery occupied the same site. Beautiful gardens surround the castle and there is a small church nearby.

From Oved take the 104 west to GETINGE and then go northeast on the E66 (also called the 15) to ROLSBERGA where you take the 23 north to BOSJOKLOSTER, one of the most picturesque castles in Sweden. Originally founded in the 12th century as a Benedictine convent, it is now a private residence of Count Thord Bonde who opens the gardens and part of the castle to the public in the summer. The castle is beautifully located on a narrow strip of land which forms a bridge across a small lake, down to which run the castle's dramatic manicured old-fashioned gardens.

From Bosjokloster, continue north towards HOOR and turn right (south) on the 105, travelling south for a few kilometers until you reach the E66 (15) where you head northeast, retracing your path through Kristianstad to Fjalkinge.

DESTINATION V BORGHOLM, Oland Island Halltorps Gastgiveri

Try to get an early start today so that you do not need to rush through the sightseeing en route. As you leave Fjalkinge, return to the E66, drive northeast to RONNEBY and take the 30 for 90 kilometers to VAXJO. Many visitors come to Sweden to visit the homeland of their parents or grandparents. If you are one of these, you will certainly not want to miss the HOUSE OF THE EMIGRANTS MUSEUM in Vaxjo and, even if your families did not come from Sweden, you will find the museum greatly interesting. Beginning in the middle of the 19th century, due to famine and financial hardships, thousands of Swedes left their homeland hoping to find a better life for themselves and their families. The museum has models of some of the ships which brought these brave people so far across the sea and archives to help emigrants search for their ancestors. There is a permanent collection called "The Dream of America" which shows the background of the emigration. It is hard to imagine, but over one-fourth of the entire Swedish population left their homeland between 1850 and 1920 - over 1.3 million people in all.

After seeing the House of Emigrants, include a visit to the SMALANDS MUSEUM. Here you will see the history of glassmaking from the very earliest times, which will fill in the background to the glass factories you will visit.

Leave Vaxjo on the 25 heading east for the 45 kilometers' drive to LESSEBO. Stop here to visit the LESSEBO PAPER MILL which dates back to the end of the 17th century and is now a museum showing how paper is made. There is a small gift shop where you can buy souvenirs. (The museum is open only during the summer months and the last tour runs at 2:15 pm.)

After seeing the paper mill, head northeast on a back road for 15 kilometers to EKEBERGA where the road intersects with the 123 and turn left (north) for the few minutes' drive to the KOSTA GLASS FACTORY. Go first to the reception area for information on the factory, then to the workshop to watch the men skillfully manipulating the molten glass into works of art. After viewing the factory you can browse through the small museum. Before leaving, be sure to visit the gift shop which is stocked with excellent values - there are many seconds (with faults so small you can sometimes not even find them) for sale at greatly reduced prices.

After visiting the Kosta factory, return to Ekeberga and turn left on a small road heading east to ORREFORS. Although short, this is a beautiful drive through dense pine forests. When you arrive at Orrefors it is easy to find the GLASS

FACTORY, which is the main industry of the town. The factory here is more modern than Kosta and the tour more sophisticated. You can view the workers from a balcony which runs around the upper level of the workroom: it is fascinating to see the beautiful forms take shape from the orange molten blobs of glass. If you are ready for a snack, visit the factory's very nice restaurant. There is also a large gift shop (where again you can purchase seconds) and an especially lovely museum.

If you have time, include the BODA GLASS FACTORY. Here you can tour the factory and also purchase wonderful souvenirs at bargain prices.

Note: These glass factories (Kosta, Orrefors and Boda) are open Monday through Friday until approximately 3:00 pm. During July they close down while the workers take their annual holiday, but there are still glass-blowing demonstrations and the gift shops and museums are open.

From Boda it is only a few minutes' drive south to the 25 where you turn left (east) for the 35-kilometer drive to KALMAR and the fabulous KALMAR CASTLE. This spectacular castle stands with mighty dignity on an island just off the coast connected to the mainland by a drawbridge - a photographer's delight. This 12th-century castle is still surrounded by its original outer wall with towers at each corner. Inside, smaller towers and turrets and gables add to the fortress-like appearance. In summer the castle is open until 4:00 pm and there are hourly tours. Of special interest are the section which was a woman's prison in the 18th century and the exhibit of objects recovered from the Kronan, a ship which sank nearby in 1676.

When you have seen the castle, follow the signs for OLAND, a long strip of island connected to Kalmar by a magnificent 6-kilometer bridge. On arriving on the island, you come almost immediately to the 136 north toward BORGHOLM.

Shortly before reaching Borgholm, you see your hotel, the HALLTORPS

GASTGIVERI, on the left side of the road. From the moment you enter the small reception area you are enveloped by the warmth of this hotel. The mood is one of country coziness - light wood country furniture, baskets of flowers, pastel walls hung with pretty pictures. Both Lars-Olof Forsberg and Josef Weichl, whose families own the hotel jointly, were restauranteurs before opening this inn and their experience is certainly obvious in the outstanding meals served. Their wives too work at the hotel, greeting guests as they arrive.

Plan to spend at least two nights in Oland as you need a minimum of one day to explore this delightful long strip of an island. The island is flat, 140 kilometers long and 16 kilometers wide: the northern portion has some pine forests while the southern portion is a limestone plain. A tour of the island holds adventure for every taste: ruins of mighty fortresses dominate the bluffs, Viking runic stones and graves stand proud, pretty little fishing villages are tucked into small coves, fabulous sand dune beaches stretch along the sea, beautiful old farmhouses stand serenely in the fields and 400 old wooden windmills full of character dot the landscape.

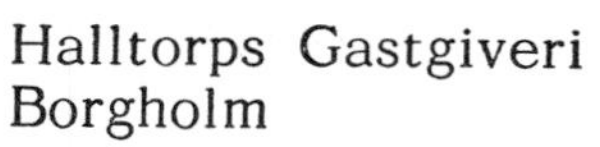

Halltorps Gastgiveri
Borgholm

HIGHLIGHTS OF OLAND ISLAND

BORGHOLM CASTLE: Stands hauntingly on the cliffs overlooking the sea. Park your car in the designated area and climb up the trail to the bluff, then meander through the silent massive shells of this once mighty fortress. The views are lovely and the remnants of yesterday awesome.

EGBY KYRKA: A tiny quaint church with a 12th-century stone altar and a baroque 18th-century pulpit.

EKETORPS BORG: The ruins of a 5th-century fortress, with walls surrounding well-preserved foundations of early homes. Archaeologists have found three different periods of history on this site and work is under way to reconstruct the fortifications.

GRABORG: The ruins of Olands's largest fortress built in elipse form. Next to the fortress stand the ruins of St. Knut's 13th-century chapel.

HIMMELSBERGA HEMBYGDSMUSEUM: A very interesting cluster of old farm buildings wonderfully furnished with rustic furniture and farm implements depicting the simple farm life of yesteryear. There is also a small gift shop and a wonderful snack shop offering fresh pastries, coffee and tea.

ISMANTORPS BORG: A short walk through the forest brings you to the circular ruins of this most interesting site. Historians are not sure of the exact purpose of this large ring of stone foundation, but, with the unusual aspect of nine entrances, it is thought this was probably a prehistoric cult site.

KAPELLUDDEN, BREDSATRA: Ruins of St. Birgitta chapel and lighthouse.

LERKAKA: Although windmills are seen everywhere on Oland, there is an especially picturesque set of five old windmills standing in a row near the road.

SODRA UDDE: An 18th-century lighthouse (with a lovely view) located on the southern tip of the island. Nearby at Ottenby there is a bird sanctuary.

SOLLIDEN: The summer residence of the Royal Family, set in the forest beside the sea just north of Borgholm. The castle is private, but during the summer the lovely parklike gardens are open to the public from noon till 2:00 pm.

DESTINATION VI SODERKOPING Soderkopings Brunn

When you leave Oland, cross back over the long bridge, drive through Kalmar and join the E66 which follows the coast northwards for the 135-kilometer drive to SODERKOPING. Make your way to the center of town and you will find your hotel, the SODERKOPINGS BRUNN, on a side canal near the square.

Soderkopings Brunn
Soderkoping

The Soderkopings Brunn originated as a spa. The ambiance is still that of a Victorian resort, with a large veranda stretching across the side of the hotel - a wonderful place for tea in the afternoon as you look out onto the gardens. This large hotel has several newer wings and an annex across the street. Only a few antiques remain to evoke the mood of yesteryear. The hotel is beautifully managed by personable Stig Ekblad (introduce yourself to him - you cannot miss Stig: he will be the tallest man in the room). The food at the Soderkopings Brunn is very good and the service excellent, but best of all is the hotel's location, set near canals and within an easy stroll of Soderkoping's extremely charming town square. Walk into the center of town to visit the 15th-century St. Lars' Church and the old schoolhouse, and let the quaint old buildings around the central square evoke memories of Soderkoping's past.

Just a short walk away is the Gota Canal, where it is great fun to watch the boats line up to wait their turn to enter the locks. Here you will see a colorful assortment of boats - and of people. Small fishing boats, beautiful sail boats, excursion boats, barges - all wait patiently to continue their journey. Families with small children, handsome young couples, groups of laughing teenage boys, weathered old men, dogs and cats complete the scene of merriment in the height of the summer season.

Soderkoping is an ideal base if you want to take some short canal excursions. In summer there is a wonderful assortment of one-day boat trips available, including those listed below:

M/S SVEA LEJON: A four-hour trip through the islands of St. Anna to the fishing hamlet of Arkosund. Two locks are navigated. Country houses, manors and the ruins of Stegeborg Castle glide past and a stop is made at the chapel of Capella Ecumenica.

M/S GOTYA LEJON: A five-hour trip that navigates 12 locks, passing through forests and meadows and by many large farms and manors.

M/S WASA LEJON: A four-hour trip that navigates a series of locks, including the last hand-operated lock in Sweden. Many small communities of 18th- and 19th-century buildings are seen along the way.

If you would like details on excursions from Soderkoping you can write to:

REDERI AB GOTA LEJON
Rederi AB Sightseeingbatar
Box 274, 60104 Norrkoping, Sweden
Tel: (011) 12 78 01

DESTINATION VII STOCKHOLM

When you leave Soderkoping take the E4 northeast through NYKOPING to the 223 which you follow for approximately 60 kilometers to the intersection with the E3. Cross the E3 and follow the signs for the short drive to the picture-perfect little village of MARIEFRED. Stop for lunch by the harbor at the GRIPSHOLMS VARDSHUS, then stroll through this quaint village enjoying the many colorful olde-worlde houses. Take a tour of GRIPSHOLM CASTLE on the small island connected to the mainland by a delightful old drawbridge. In addition to being extremely photogenic, the castle houses the world's largest collection of portraits.

From Mariefred, return to the E3 and follow the freeway into Stockholm to tie in with another itinerary or to travel on to your next destination by ship, plane, train or car.

Oslo to Bergen Via Fjords & Farms

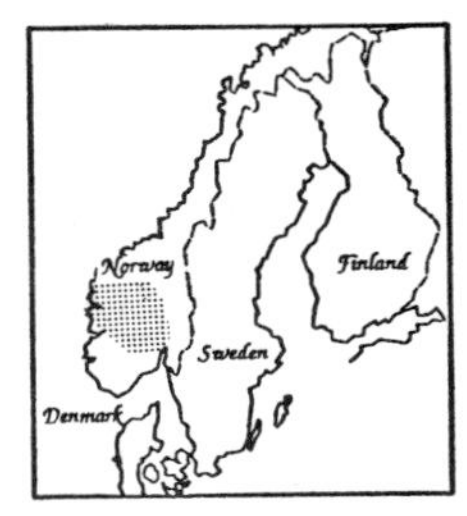

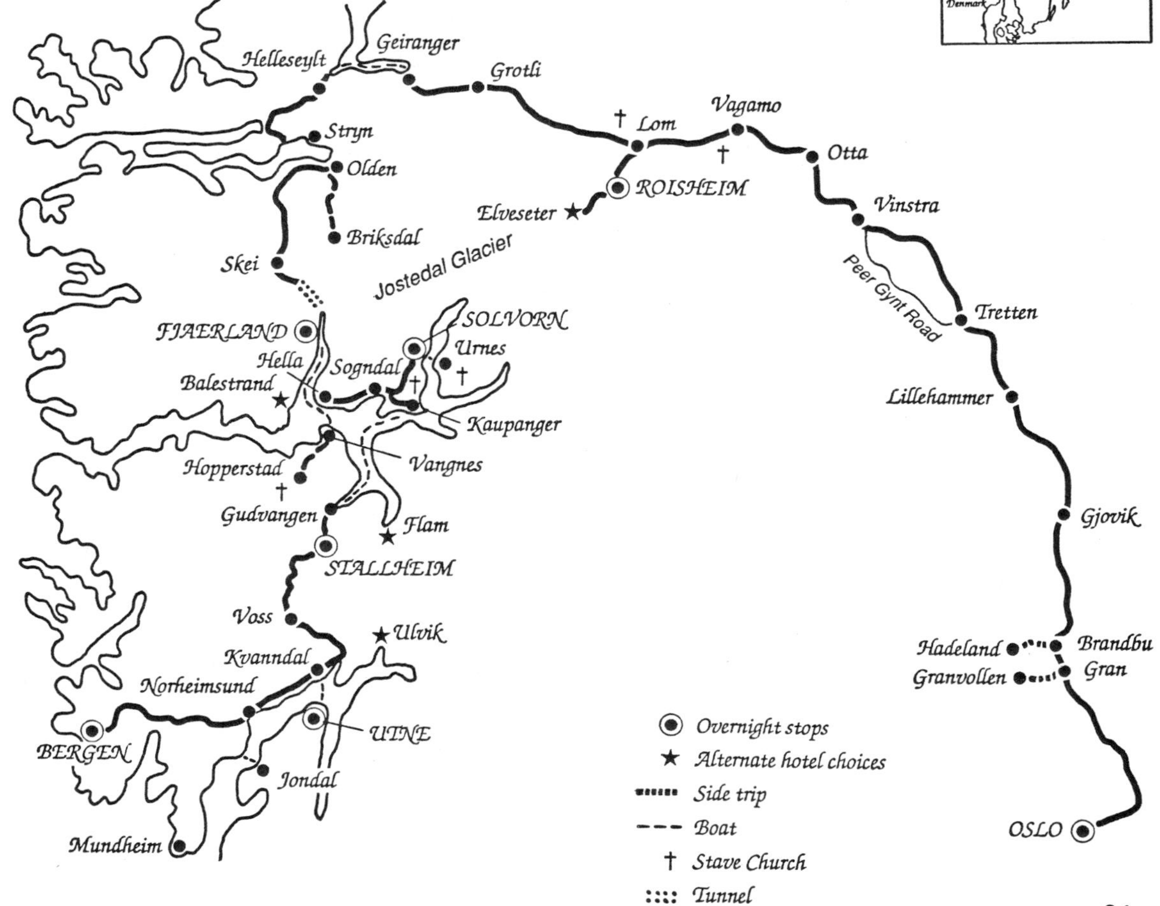

Oslo to Bergen Via Fjords & Farms

The majestic beauty of Norway can be described only with superlatives. From the barren rocks of the north to the high mountains in the south, Norway's beauty is astounding; almost too beautiful to be reai. But, most spectacular of all, and unique to Norway, are the fabulous fjords, particularly those that surround Bergen. This itinerary links the two most popular cities of Norway, Oslo and Bergen, but, instead of taking the usual direct route, loops through gorgeous valleys, wiggles in and out of breathtaking fjords, and frequently hops across the water by crawling into the jaws of giant ferry boats. Included along the way are the Geirangerfjord, the Sognefjord and the Hardangerfjord, the beauty of each savored both from the snug comfort of a ferry lounge and through the windows of your car. Along the way, whether it be in lush valleys, beside silent fjords, or beneath glacier-tipped mountains, you see numerous farms - tucked everywhere from the ledges of soaring mountains to tiny patches clinging beside the fjords.

Lom Stave Church

In every possible niche, and some that seem impossible, the clever Norwegians have carved out a place to grow their crops and graze their goats and cows. The farms' facades change with the landscape, from gigantic red barns outlined in white trim to compact log barns with roofs of sod. The trees are ever present - forests are everywhere and trees lace the countryside. So do not whiz directly between Oslo and Bergen: instead linger along the way, enjoying some of the highlights of Norway's beauty and staying in some of her friendliest little inns.

ORIGINATING CITY OSLO

OSLO offers many opportunities for sightseeing in the city itself or for wonderful excursions into the countryside which can easily be made in a day using Oslo as your "base". Pages 27 to 30 cover sightseeing suggestions. Plan your time according to what most appeals to you before heading north into the countryside.

DESTINATION I LOM Roisheim Hotel

Plan to have a hearty breakfast and get an early start this morning because a five-hour drive lies ahead of you, an even longer trip if you stop for sightseeing along the way. The most direct route is highway 4. As you leave the city behind, you pass through several suburban towns and then are in the countryside. Most of the sightseeing today is in the natural beauty of the landscape, but there are a few other sightseeing possibilities for those who want to "see everything". About 70 kilometers north from Oslo on the 4, just before you come to the town of GRAN, there is a small road to the left marked to GRANVOLLEN which is a small village in the hills above Gran (about a ten-minute drive). Here you will find the SISTER CHURCHES which, according to legend, were built by two sisters: the oldest is the small Maria Church. After seeing the churches, return to Gran and continue on the 4 for the short drive to BRANDBU. As the road comes into town, there is a sign to the left to the HADELAND FOLKS MUSEUM. Again, the road winds up the hill to the folk museum which has 24 restored buildings brought from around the area. There is also a small museum which has an excellent exhibit of antique handicrafts with examples of beautiful handwoven linen, lovingly enhanced with intricate needlecraft by the local women. (The best bonus of this little museum is the delightful lady who is the guide and the "keeper of the keys". She will show you around the museum and add tidbits of local history about this part of Norway.) After seeing the folk museum, return to Brandbu and continue north on the 4 until you reach GJOVIK. From here the road follows the lake and takes you to the industrial town of LILLEHAMMER. A few kilometers southeast of Lillehammer is the MAIHAUGEN OPEN-AIR MUSEUM, a large park with 120 restored buildings characteristic of the Gudbrandsdal Valley.

At Lillehammer the 4 joins highway 6 as you continue north. About half an hour after leaving Lillehammer you arrive in TRETTEN where there is a sign showing a possible alternate route going north via the PEER GYNT ROAD. Avid Ibsen enthusiasts may want to take this more rugged road through the countryside where the legendary Peer Gynt lived, although the driving conditions are very bad and the landscape very wild. Much more highly recommended is to continue north on the 6 through the GUDBRANDDALEN - a beautiful drive tracing the Losna River as it winds its way through the valley where lovely white farmhouses and enormous red barns accentuate the lush green meadows. Sometimes the valley is very narrow, sometimes wide and gentle - but always picturesque.

Continue on the 6 until you reach the town of OTTA and then follow the well-marked signs for highway 15 heading west. In about 20 minutes you come to the town of VAGAMO where you should stop to see the STAVE CHURCH, easy to spot to the left of the road in the center of the village. A further 45-minute drive brings you to LOM. Watch for the sign for highway 55 where you turn left and head south through a narrow, high mountain valley, rugged and splendid. The road follows a small river trapped between mountains and you see old farmhouses of darkened logs with marvelous sod roofs dotting the valley sides.

Roisheim Hotel
Lom

A short drive brings you to one of these farms, the ROISHEIM HOTEL, a special little inn incorporated into farm buildings dating back to the 17th century. This is one of the most charming inns in Norway. There are only a few bedrooms with private bathrooms, but each guestroom has a different decor, with country Pierre Dieux-style fabrics and wood floors with colorful throw rugs. Some of the bedrooms have a few antiques, but most have simple painted beds and chests. For those who enjoy walking there are trails in every direction and you see hardy Norwegians tramping out each morning, rain or shine, with their slickers and sturdy shoes. On a rainy day, retire to the cozy antique-filled lounge with a roaring fire - a perfect place to curl up with a good book. In the evenings there is always a delicious dinner in the beautiful small dining room. Wilfried Reinschmidt who owns this inn with his lovely wife Unni is a gourmet cook.

It will be difficult to leave Roisheim, and when you do, it will be like saying goodbye to friends as you bid Unni and Wilfried farewell. However, some of the most gorgeous scenery in the world awaits you; the Norwegian fjords. Your first destination is GEIRANGER and from there you take the ferry to HELLESEYLT. The distance from Lom to Geiranger is only about 150 kilometers, but get an early start so that you have plenty of time to stop along the way to absorb the vistas and also to allow time in Geiranger for lunch before the boat leaves.

Retrace your steps to Lom and head west along the 15. Almost immediately you see on the right side of the road the beautiful LOM STAVE CHURCH. Make a quick stop for photographs because, with the mountains in the background, this church is immensely photogenic. A short drive brings you to SKJAK, famous as the accordian district in Norway (also supposed to be as dry as the Sahara Desert - although this is hard to believe). The scenery becomes drier and harsher as you continue west where desolate moorlands sweep upward, stretching to the mountains which slumber beneath white glacier blankets. You pass through GROTLI, for many years a favorite mountain pass stopping place, now a summer training spot for cross country skiers. About 15 minutes beyond Grotli there is an intersection where you take highway 58 north following the signs for Geiranger. Climbing in gentle loops, you cross a high mountain pass which is most dramatic. At first the land is severe yet beautiful: waterfalls leap from high cliffs and glaciers loom in the distance. In summer various shades of moss and wildflowers cling to the rocky terrain. After reaching the summit, the road plunges down the mountain in a series of sharp hairpin turns. Suddenly the landscape changes, lush farmland appears and in the distance the gorgeous GEIRANGERFJORD pops into view. Little farms dot the valley, with enormous cliffs soaring on each side. Strategic niches are located along the road so that you can safely stop to enjoy one of the most justly famous panoramas in the world as the Geirangerfjord comes into view below you.

Follow signs through Geiranger for the HELLESEYLT FERRY. Go directly to the ferry and secure your place in the queue. Once your place in line is established you can leave your car and have lunch or browse through the small tourist shop next to the dock. About 15 minutes before the ferry leaves, the ferry agent orchestrates the placement of each vehicle as it drives into the boat's giant jaws.

1:15 pm leave Geiranger by ferry
2:15 pm arrive Helleseylt.

After your car rolls off the ferry, drive up the hill to highway 60. Turn left and follow signs to STRYN. The road winds over a small pass and then down again to lush farmland before arriving about an hour later in Stryn. The 60 follows the shoreline around the INNVIKFJORD - a perfectly beautiful drive where a tantalizing vista presents itself at every turn. It will probably be about 3:30 pm by the time you reach OLDEN, one of the villages along the Innvikfjord. It will make your day a very long one, but there is a side trip from Olden that is too special not to mention. So, if it is a perfect day, and if you would like an extra adventure, watch for signposts to BRIKSDALBREEN. This road winds back into one of the most glorious valleys in Norway, tracing the shoreline of two gemlike lakes. At times the road is no more than a bike path, then it widens a bit, only to become even more narrow afterwards. After the second lake, the road follows a river into the end of the valley where the BRIKSDAL GLACIER pours over the mountain, suspended above the valley floor. Near the parking area at the foot of the glacier are a pension, a gift shop and a small restaurant. There are also horses and buggies waiting to take those who so desire to "meet" the glacier. The roundtrip to the glacier by horse and buggy takes two hours, so there really is no way you can work this in. However, since your hotel for the night faces the other side of the Briksdal Glacier, you will have time to view it another day.

From Olden, continue along the 60 as it curves beside the fjord. When you reach UTVIK the road leaves the water and heads south over a small pass to BYRKJELO and then on to SKEI. At Skei leave the 60 and turn left onto the 625 to FJAERLAND. This road traces the shore of a small fjord and then ducks into the new 6-kilometer tunnel - a real engineering feat. When you emerge from the tunnel, you are only a few minutes from Fjaerland, a beautiful hamlet hugging the shore of one of Norway's most picturesque fjords, a small narrow branch of the Sognefjord. Across the street from the water is the HOTEL MUNDAL, a charming Victorian-style, white building dating from 1891. Marit Mauritzen, whose grandfather built the hotel, operates this wonderful old inn with such a gracious warmth you think you are a guest in a private home. The decor is simple, with a homey comfort. Although old-fashioned in decor, the Hotel Mundal is run with sophistication and the food is fabulous.

Hotel Mundal
Fjaerland

Fjaerland is the kind of town to savor and enjoy, so try to spend a few days here. This hamlet, tucked at the end of the Fjaerland Fjord, is truly one of the most beautiful places in Norway: the mountains rise in a series of enormous green peaks - like a Peter Pan fantasy - while behind the mountains lies the

JOSTEDAL GLACIER. The little row of houses lining the shore reflect in the still waters of the fjord and two small rowboats are docked in front of the hotel's garden, waiting for guests to go fishing. Glorious paths beckon in every direction; two arms of the Jostedal Glacier are just a ten-minute drive away; bird watching is supreme. All in all, this is a marvelous place to escape to. This idyllic little hideaway seems like a far corner of the world - yet the world is not so big: former Vice President Walter Mondale's grandfather emigrated from Fjaerland to America in 1856. (Mr Mondale returned to Norway in the summer of 1986 to officially open the spectacular new tunnel into Fjaerland.)

DESTINATION III SOLVORN Walaker Hotel

Note: It is possible to eliminate this stopover in Solvorn by taking the 2:45 pm ferry from KAUPANGER to GUDVANGEN and driving directly to STALHEIM. But in doing so you miss two exceptionally interesting stave churches and a touch of homespun, genuine Norwegian hospitality at the Walaker Hotel.

The first leg of your journey today is the ferry from Fjaerland to HELLA:

11:00 am leave Fjaerland by ferry
12:15 pm arrive Hella

Upon arrival in Hella, drive your car from the ferry and almost immediately make a U turn to board the ferry for VANGSNES.

12:25 pm leave Hella by ferry
12:40 pm arrive Vangsnes

After disembarking, follow the 13 in the direction of VOSS. It is only 12 kilometers to VIK. Drive right through the town and just on the outskirts you see the sign for a road on the right to the HOPPERSTAD STAVE CHURCH. This is the second oldest stave church in Norway, occupying an especially lovely site atop its own tiny hill in the midst of a pretty valley. The church was in disrepair when a wealthy Norwegian spared no expense to have it meticulously restored. The inside is delightful and there is usually a friendly guide on hand whose romantic stories make your visit even more memorable.

After visiting the church, return to Vangsnes and take the ferry back to Hella. As you wait for the boat, you can have lunch at the snack bar near the pier.

2:15 pm leave Vangsnes by ferry
2:30 pm arrive Hella

When your ferry arrives in Hella, follow highway 55 east to SOGNDAL. You travel first along the fjord then through a forest as the road heads inland over a low pass. About 15 minutes beyond Sogndal, the road is signposted to the right for SOLVORN, only a few minutes farther. Solvorn is just a cluster of Victorian houses, including the WALAKER HOTEL, set around the harbor. The Walaker Hotel is a very simple, unsophisticated family hotel, but with an incredible history: the same family has owned the property since 1690. It has not always been a hotel: during its rich history it has been a farm, a postal station and a bakery, and, in recent times, was confiscated by the Nazis who kept the family virtual prisoners in their own home. Fortunately, the inn has been receiving guests again for many years. One section is a rather stark motel, but the heart of the hotel is a delightful small white old-fashioned inn, entered through a fragrant flower garden. The decor in the parlor exudes a cluttered, fussy, Victorian homespun warmth: this is the gathering place where guests mingle by the fire to exchange stories of their day's adventures or join in song by the piano. The guestrooms are simple, but if you ask for a room in front, the view of the fjord is blissfully serene. The Walaker family is a delight: Oda is your gracious hostess and Hermod the chef who makes each meal a treat.

Walaker Hotel
Solvorn

While you are in Solvorn you must visit the URNES STAVE CHURCH. This excursion is easy to arrange - there are ferries which make the 15-minute run across the channel of the fjord to URNES. Or, if you miss the ferry, Oda Walaker will call a boat taxi which picks you up at the pier and brings you home again. As you ride across the fjord you can see the tiny spire of the church pointing up between the trees on the hillside. After docking, it is about a 20-minute walk up the hillside, through farms and apple trees, to the church. This tiny jewel of a church is very interesting, not only because of its intricate engravings, but also because it is the oldest stave church in Norway. Usually when you arrive the custodian of the keys is waiting there, ready to tell you all about the church for a small fee. If not, she lives in the farmhouse adjacent to the path.

There are several other excursions you can take to see more of the Jostedal Glacier, or, if you want to just relax, there is a nice path which winds through the forest near the hotel where you can pick a bouquet of wildflowers as you stroll.

When it is time to leave Solvorn, return to Sogndal and turn left at the large bridge, just as you enter town, following the 5 towards KAUPANGER. It is only about another 15 minutes to Kaupanger. As the town approaches, keep watch on the right side of the road for the KAUPANGER STAVE CHURCH, which you can see from the road: it makes a pretty picture with the fjord in the background. The church is usually locked but you can walk around the outside before driving on into town to the pier where you take the ferry to Gudvangen.

2:45 pm leave Kaupanger by ferry
5:05 pm arrive Gudvangen

The ferry leaves the pier at Kaupanger and crosses the fjord to stop briefly for more passengers at Revsnes before continuing west. In about an hour the ferry turns into the AURLANDSFJORD, a branch of the Sognefjord. About an hour and a half after leaving Kaupanger, a most remarkable event takes place: at a junction of the fjord, where one branch goes to Flam and the other to Kaupanger, the ferry pulls next to a sister ship, a ramp is quickly slung between the two, and passengers are exchanged. Then your ferry makes a turn to the right and weaves down a narrow ribbon of waterway toward Gudvangen while the other ferry continues on the alternate branch toward Flam. Only the Norwegians could devise such an efficient solution to transferring passengers.

As your ferry follows the curves of the fjord, you witness some of the most breathtaking scenery in Norway. Superlatives are inadequate. The green hills drop like curtains of velvet on either side of the boat - so close you almost feel you could stretch your arms and touch each side. Occasionally a tiny farm appears, snuggled onto a patch of land far above the water. A tall church spire announces a tiny village nestled at the waterside, locked in by water with boat its only means of access. The green walls change to gray as granite cliffs, too steep for vegetation, tower powerfully overhead. All too soon, the small town of GUDVANGEN appears at the tip of the fjord and the journey ends.

As you drive off the boat, the road follows a sparkling little river through the valley and then begins to climb up into the cone-like, gigantic mountains. The road climbs steadily upwards and you catch views of the STALHEIM HOTEL, perched impossibly high in the clouds above you on a ledge of the cliff. The turnoff to the hotel is well-marked.

Stalheim Hotel
Stalheim

The Stalheim Hotel is neither old nor tiny, but it has one of the most dazzling locations of any hotel in Norway, a location so special that a stopover here is certainly justified. And although the hotel is new and modern in construction, the history of the hotel dates back over 100 years to the time when a wonderful old Victorian inn stood on the site. Unfortunately, it burned down, as did a subsequent hotel. The latest replacement is a long, red, modern building stretched across the bluff overlooking the valley below as it snakes its way between mountains almost too picturesque to believe. There are many tours that use this hotel, but fortunately its creative owner has maintained the warmth and friendliness of a small inn. The staff is exceptional and you never feel lost in a mass of humanity. Moreover, although the hotel is modern, Mr Tonneberg, the owner, has an outstandingly fine collection of antiques which are tastefully incorporated into the decor. There is an open-air museum on a hillock above the hotel where Mr. Tonneberg again demonstrates his respect for the traditional old Norwegian heritage: here many houses particular to this region have been reconstructed and furnished in the appropriate style. But it is the view that captures the imagination, so splurge, request a deluxe room with a spectacular view.

DESTINATION V UTNE Utne Hotel

No need to rush this morning because it is a short drive then a brief ferry ride to tonight's destination. You might want to enjoy one of the famous lunches served at the Stalheim Hotel - and then linger on the terrace enjoying the view. From the Stalheim Hotel take the E68 downhill as it weaves through the forest beside a beautiful river. Soon more civilization appears as you near the town of VOSS, one of the main hubs of rail traffic between Bergen and Oslo.

From Voss, continue on the E68 following signs for BERGEN. For about 15 minutes you follow the railroad as it winds through the trees, then suddenly there beneath you, as the road begins to make giant loops downward, is a perfectly glorious valley, hemmed in on both sides by grey walls of granite. To further enhance the scene, a giant waterfall leaps from far above the highway, crashing to the rocks below, and then gushes through a tunnel under the road to continue its dash down to the valley below. Continue along the shoreline of the GRAANVINFJORD until you reach KVANNDAL where you leave the highway to join the cars at the pier lining up for the 15-minute boat ride to UTNE.

The UTNE HOTEL, conveniently located across from the dock, is easy to spot as your boat crosses the narrow fjord. Leaving the ferry, just drive across the road and park in the designated area to the left of the hotel.

Utne Hotel
Utne

The Utne Hotel, dating back to 1722, is the oldest inn in Norway, and, from the moment you arrive, you are greeted with old-fashioned hospitality by the charming owner, Hildegun Aga Blokhus, whose family has owned this small hotel for 200 years. The bedrooms are all simple, but the lounges and small parlor are filled with antiques and offer a cozy, comfy ambiance. This is the kind of hotel where you feel like a guest rather than a customer. Rainy days find the patrons reading a good book or struggling over a puzzle in front of the fire with a cup of tea. If possible stay a few days, for not only is the food superb and the atmosphere snug, but there are many excursions you can make to other villages on the fjord just by walking across the street to the ferry. During summer there is a gloriously beautiful excursion by boat to the idyllic town of ULVIK where you can enjoy lunch at the BRAKANES HOTEL. About a 20-minute drive from Utne, in the direction of Odda, is the tiny village of AGA. This whole town is so old that it is a museum, not like most outdoor museums so frequently seen in Norway where the buildings have been brought to the site and reconstructed -

this village has always been just where you see it now. Utnes itself is a delight - just a stroll from the hotel is a museum displaying many of the traditional costumes plus some beautifully decorated fiddles - a specialty of the Hardanger area.

DESTINATION VI BERGEN

When it is time to leave Utne there are several choices for your drive to Bergen. The shortest route is to cross the fjord from Utne to Kvanndal and take the E68 directly into Bergen. However, if it is a beautiful bright day, you can plot the route on your map and wind your way back through and over the fjords via JONDAL and MUNDHEIM and take the southern route to Bergen.

BERGEN, nestling along the banks of one of the arms of the Byfjord, is one of Europe's most appealing cities. One of the joys of Bergen is exploring on your own since there are so many delights to discover and picturesque scenes to absorb. One of the most colorful is the row of brightly painted wooden houses, dating from the Hanseatic period, which line the harbor - a picture-postcard scene. Also a photographer's dream is the market place at the tip of the harbor where fishmongers sell their day's catch and flower stalls burst with bloom. The tourist office in the center of town has an excellent selection of tours available which leave from beside the office. In the "Highlights of Scandinavia" itinerary, further information and suggestions are given for sightseeing, beginning on page 20.

Before leaving Bergen, you might want to extend your vacation by taking the coastal steamer which leaves daily for the 12-day round trip adventure to the north of Norway. See page 103 for details of this itinerary.

Fantastic Fjords of Norway - Daytrips from Bergen

All of Norway is a fairyland of incredible beauty, but if you must choose just one area to see, visit her fjords. These offer some of the most spectacular scenery in all the world. To visit Norway without experiencing the fjord country would be like enjoying a delectable meal but forgetting the dessert. Fortunately, the fjord country is easily accessible from Bergen and the transportation system so superbly geared that you can stay in Bergen and take daytrips to see the fjords. The following outings use Bergen as your base and return there each night. (For sightseeing suggestions in Bergen refer to pages 20-22). Visiting the fjords is easy and the different forms of transport that you use make each excursion a memorable adventure. The Bergen Tourist Center, Torgalmenning, 5000 Bergen, tel: (05) 32 14 80, has several booklets on Bergen and fjord excursions that outline briefly these and other do-it-yourself daytrips. The center can explain how to obtain tickets and any necessary seat reservations. Each daytrip offers a slightly different perspective. Times are given to assist you with planning, but remember: schedules change, so double check them.

Sognefjord

Norway in a Nutshell

9:10	am	leave Bergen by train
11:20	am	arrive Mydral
11:45	am	leave Mydral by train
12:38	pm	arrive Flam
2:30	pm	leave Flam by ferry
4:35	pm	arrive Gudvangen
5:00	pm	leave Gudvangen by bus
6:30	pm	arrive Voss
7:10	pm	leave Voss by train
8:35	pm	arrive Bergen

Operates daily - June to August

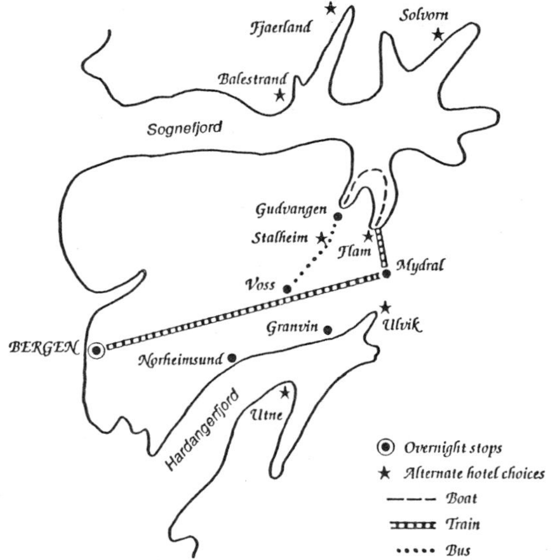

This trip is indeed advertised as "Norway in a Nutshell". For those who want to squeeze the maximum scenery into a day's excursion, this is a splendid outing. The train ride from Bergen's Central Station to MYDRAL is glorious, but the real treat awaits you on the connecting train from Mydral to Flam. This is a railway journey known to train buffs the world over: the colorful red train chugs away from Mydral into a panorama of ever-changing countryside. It weaves through 20 tunnels and twists down a mountain pass before making its way to the valley below. The sympathetic driver pauses at the most spectacular vistas and gives time to hop out to take photographs. (See page 25 for more details.)

All too quickly the train rolls into the lush Flam Valley and follows the crystal-clear rushing river to FLAM, a beautifully situated village on the edge of the fjord. In Flam you can enjoy a picnic of sandwiches purchased from one of the snack-stands or a more formal lunch at the FRETHEIM HOTEL. This hotel is recommended for those who wish to break their journey and overnight here. When it is time to leave, you can easily spot your steamer because it it pulls into the harbor within easy sight of the train station. The boat takes you along two of the most beautiful tiny fjords in Norway, small branches of the Sognefjord.

Leaving Flam, the ferry threads through the AURLANDSFJORD, makes a left turn and continues down the even more beautiful NAEROYFJORD whose walls of granite rise majestically on either side of the very narrow fjord. All too soon you see the village of GUDVANGEN nestled in the valley at the fjord's head. From here a dramatic bus ride awaits. First the bus follows the beautiful, verdant Gudvangen Valley, and then loops up around a series of hairpin curves, through a tunnel and across the mountains to VOSS where it pulls up in front of the railway station where you board the train back to Bergen. This trip might sound hectic, but it is not: all the transportation is carefully coordinated so it is an easy transition from train to boat to bus to train.

Mydral-Flam Train

Sognefjord and the Flam Valley

7:30	am	leave Bergen by hydrofoil
1:50	pm	arrive Flam
3:25	pm	leave Flam by train
4:10	pm	arrive Mydral
4:31	pm	leave Mydral by train
6:55	pm	arrive Bergen

Operates daily - June to August

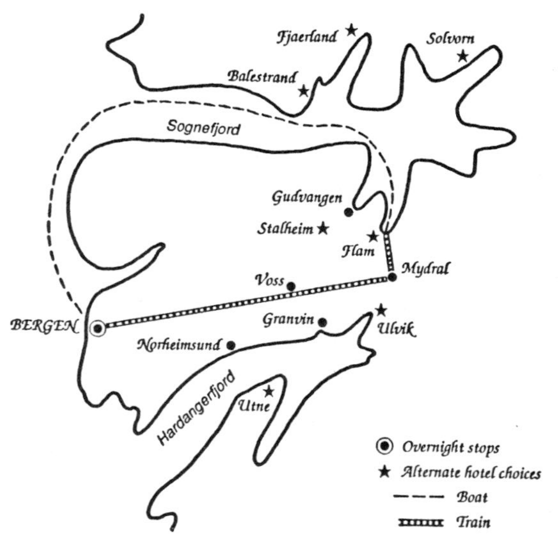

The hydrofoil, which is the first leg of this do-it-yourself tour, departs from the harbor in Bergen. With your vessel skimming across the water it presents beautiful scenery as it passes between many little islands and heads north up the coast, dips into the SOGNEFJORD and ends its journey in Flam. (The HOTEL FRETHEIM is suggested for those who wish to overnight here.) The second part of this itinerary is the sensational train ride from FLAM to MYDRAL (described in detail beginning page 25), connecting with a train to Bergen.

Minicruise on the Hardangerfjord

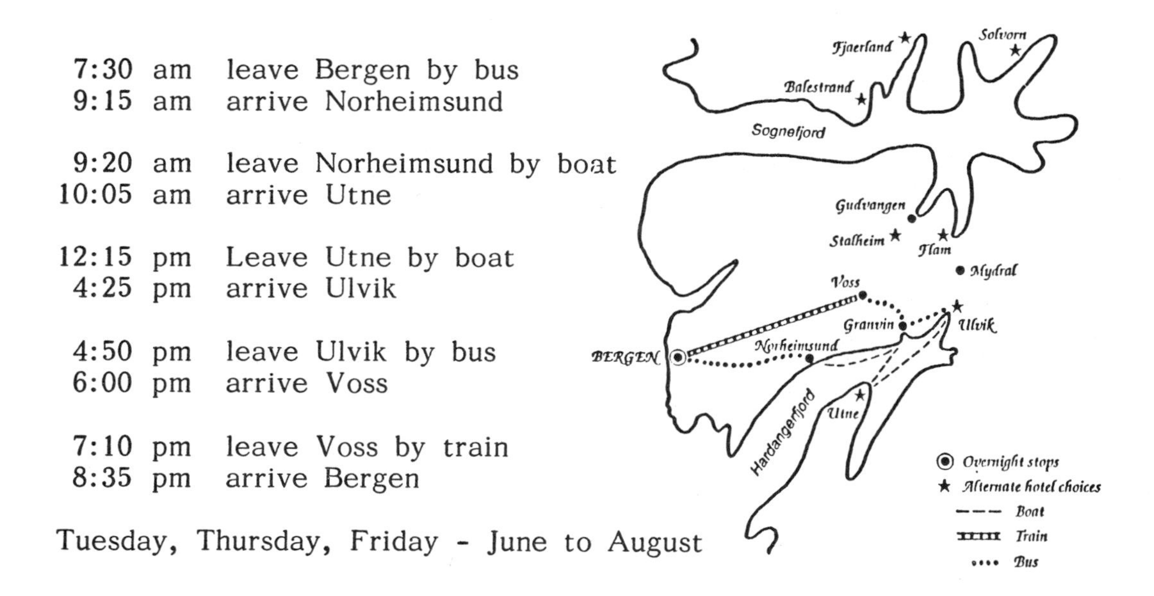

7:30	am	leave Bergen by bus
9:15	am	arrive Norheimsund
9:20	am	leave Norheimsund by boat
10:05	am	arrive Utne
12:15	pm	Leave Utne by boat
4:25	pm	arrive Ulvik
4:50	pm	leave Ulvik by bus
6:00	pm	arrive Voss
7:10	pm	leave Voss by train
8:35	pm	arrive Bergen

Tuesday, Thursday, Friday - June to August

The HARDANGERFJORD, one of the most spectacular fjords in Norway, originates south of Bergen, winding its way inland over 100 kilometers. The Sognefjord (mentioned in the two previous itineraries) with its steep granite walls is perhaps a bit more dramatic than the Hardangerfjord, but the Hardangerfjord is also gorgeous in a gentler, more serene way. It too has many narrow straits and romantic mountains rising steeply from the water's edge, but in the Hardangerjford, the rocky cliffs are softened by hospitable patches of land where beautiful apple orchards flourish. Each of these fjords is truly glorious ... each has its own unique beauty. Try to include them both while in Bergen.

Should you prefer to extend your outing to more than one day, this itinerary lends itself especially well to overnighting in ULVIK, a beautiful little town tucked at the tip of a very narrow branch of the Hardangerfjord. In Ulvik, the BRAKANES HOTEL has the prize position - right on the water with a lawn rolling down to its own small dock. Although the hotel dates back to the 19th century, it was burned to the ground in World War II by the Germans who fired on it from a ship in the harbor. As a result, the hotel had to be completely rebuilt. Although the hotel is new and slickly commercial, its views are some of the finest in Norway.

If you overnight in Ulvik you can enjoy a day of stunning scenery by taking the bus to GUDVANGEN, ferry to FLAM, the mountain railway to MYDRAL, the train to VOSS and the bus back to Ulvik. (This excursion from Ulvik is similar to "Norway in a Nutshell" described on page 98.)

Another choice for a truly "off beat" excursion from Ulvik is to explore the fjord further aboard the M/S GRANVIN. This little milkboat operates year round, on Tuesdays and Thursdays. It departs from Ulvik at 11:45 am, makes short stops at farms along the fjord (some not accessible by road) and arrives in GRANVIN at 4:15 pm. The bus leaves Granvin at 6:20 pm and arrives in Ulvik at 6:55 pm - just in time for supper.

Norway's Colorful Coastal Steamer

Norway's Colorful Coastal Steamer

Every day of the year a giant coastal steamer quietly pulls out of the Bergen harbor to begin its 12-day roundtrip journey north across the Arctic Circle and almost to the Russian border where the ship turns around at Kirkenes to retrace its way back to Bergen. For many years this coastal steamer was the only link with civilization that many of the tiny coastal hamlets north of Bergen enjoyed. Today, airports dot Norway's northern coast and modern concrete bridges span wide gaps of water, making the world accessible to these remote areas. However, even today the steamers are the key transportation and communication for northern Norway. Some of the small towns are still without roads and even those with airports are dependent upon hospitable weather for the airplanes to land, so the daily steamer is still almost as important as in bygone days.

As soon as the ship slips into each village and pulls up to the dock, enormous cranes swing into motion, lowering and lifting bags of mail and supplies for the community. While the cranes swing out, the ramp is released for passengers to disembark before boarding those waiting on the pier, for people are one of the basic "cargos" carried on the ships. Up the ramp comes a joyful assortment: mothers with apple-cheeked blond children - probably on their way to visit their grandparents at a nearby town; groups of noisy schoolchildren patiently quieted by their teacher on their way to a day's excursion; many teenagers, frequently with their bicyles, on their way to school; elderly couples, sometimes with their dog trotting along by their side on a leash, going to visit their children. Happily, it is not only the "natives" who can use the coastal steamers for transportation. Anyone can make a reservation for this scenic journey.

Should you want to take advantage of this colorful steamer to visit the coastal villages of northern Norway, you can buy your ticket and board at any of the ports of call, then disembark at your will. There is a cafeteria aboard where you can purchase meals and snacks. If you are extremely adventurous (or young and hearty) and do not mind sleeping each night in a chair, you can take this trip without cabin reservations, but for the most comfort and enjoyment, you will need to reserve staterooms well in advance (sometimes almost a year). Although a ship leaves Bergen every morning, the cabins are very popular, not only with Americans, but especially with the British who love the adventure of seeing Norway by sea. The Bergen Lines in the United States represents the Coastal Cruises and your travel agent can handle the reservation for you.

The roundtrip voyage takes 12 days to weave its way up the west coast, cross the Arctic Circle, circle the northern tip of Norway and return to Bergen. If your vacation time is limited, you can begin the trip in Bergen and disembark in Kirkenes where you can then fly on to your next destination. (Or, of course, do the reverse - fly to Kirkenes and then board the ship for the six-day trip back to Bergen.) Although as you look at the itinerary below you will notice that most of the towns are repeated in each direction, the roundtrip journey is still not a duplicate of experience because some of the villages are visited in the wee hours of the morning. Also, different shore excursions are offered in each direction. However, you can certainly get a "feel" of the journey and even half a trip is well worthwhile if your time is limited.

This journey is definitely for those with a love of the sea and a sense of adventure. In no way can these ships be compared with luxury cruises, but fun they are. Although you can book any season of the year, summer is the time to cruise when the days are long, the seas more gentle and the weather warmer. Plus, in summer the ships are geared toward tourists with planned excursions and a hostess on board. As you board the ship there is a simple desk in the lobby where you are greeted and shown to one of the cabins, all of which are small and almost all with only upper and lower berths. Most ships have cabins with private showers, but the bathrooms are extremely tiny and become totally wet when you bathe. Nevertheless, the beds are comfortable and everything is spotlessly clean. Each ship has several lounges and a cafeteria where food can be bought anytime of the day. For those with cabin reservations, there is a dining room where meals are served in two sittings. You will be assigned a place in the dining room - probably sharing a table with other passengers. At each meal there is a large buffet table where you can help yourself, while at dinner there is a choice of entrees which will be served to you. As you might expect, fish is standard fare, as are potatoes, vegetables and salads. The food is not fancy, but there is plenty of it and, after a day in the fresh air, everything tastes wonderful.

This is not a dressy voyage so no formal wear is needed - just comfortable slacks or skirts and sweaters. Even in the summertime you should bring warm clothes: you might be lucky and have bright sunshine, but usually the days are chilly and there is a lot of rain. In the winter, the days are short and the weather can be bitterly cold as the Arctic winds gust.

During the summer season a hostess accompanies each sailing. These are usually extremely gracious, very capable, attractive young Norwegians. Their duties are unending as they are there to assist in anything the passengers might want to do. Many travellers on board curl up with a good book or share conversation with fellow passengers (there is a definite camaraderie aboard and friends are quickly made), but for those desiring more structured pastimes, the hostess will help set up bridge or other games. In addition, the hostess takes reservations for the various shore excursions and joins the group as the bus departs for sightseeing. There are many excursions offered along the way: definitely try to take them all so that you can squeeze the most out of your adventure. The hostess also arranges various special events such as movies and costume parties.

This itinerary is the basic route that all the coastal steamers follow. The 35 ports of call are not individually described in detail because, quite honestly, most are similar villages - a cluster of colorfully painted houses hugging the harbor. The ports of call are usually brief, but the amount of time allocated at each stop is posted and passengers are free to disembark, browse around the tiny villages and do a bit of shopping. (Speaking of shopping, bring any bottle of liquor you want with you since it is impossible to buy any in most of the stops along the way.) There is very little left in the way of old wooden construction since what was not destroyed by fire over the years was devastated by the Germans before they departed after World War II. However, although newly built, most of the towns are colorful, with houses painted brightly in all shades of blues and yellows and pinks - probably to maintain a brightness of mood during long drab winters. The scenery is beautiful as the ship leaves Bergen, with a heavily forested coastline constantly broken by deep fjords. As the ship plies north, gradually the trees give way to barren rocks and rugged hills.

DAY I

Just before midnight the Coastal Steamer pulls out of the Bergen harbor making its way north through the archipelago. There are no stops until dawn.

DAY II

The first call in the morning is FLORO and then MALOY, an important fishing center with many canning and refrigeration plants. The next stop is ALESUND, Norway's largest fishing port which is famous for its fleet of ships which catch halibut, herring, shark and cod. Then on to MOLDE, beautifully situated facing a fjord with a panorama of 87 snow-capped mountain peaks. A bus is waiting on the pier for those who have signed up for the optional overland excursion to KRISTIANSUND where dinner will be served in town before the group rejoins the ship. Kristiansund is a picturesque town with wooden houses built in terraces stepping up from the harbor.

DAY III

The ship arrives early in the morning in TRONDHEIM, one of Norway's most charming cities. Founded in 997 by the Viking King Olav, Trondheim maintains a wonderful olde-worlde ambiance. There is a shore excursion to RINGVE MANOR HOUSE to see the excellent museum of musical instruments. Coffee and cake are served before the bus returns for the passengers to reboard the ship. The last call for the day is RORVIK, where fishing, net mending, and a seaweed processing factory are the main sources of commerce.

DAY IV

This morning the ship crosses the Arctic Circle, then soon arrives at the small town of ORNES. Another optional shore excursion is available and a bus will be waiting to take passengers overland to meet the ship in BODO. In the evening the ship arrives at STAMSUND for a brief stay and then on to SVOLVAER.

DAY V

Early in the morning the ship arrives in HARSTAD, an important trading center, and then moves on to FINNSNES, located on a small promontory sticking out into the channel. In the mid-afternoon TROMSO comes into view on a small island. Many polar expeditions have begun at Tromso which is considered the capital of northern Norway. There is an optional shore excursion in Tromso which takes visitors to the top of the mountain by cable car, or, if the weather is poor, to visit a museum. After leaving Tromso, the ship stops briefly at SKJERVOY.

DAY VI

Midmorning the ship arrives in HONNINGSVAG where there is an optional excursion by bus to the NORTH CAPE. Warm jackets, cap and gloves are recommended for this excursion. At the summit there is a restaurant where sandwiches and hot coffee are available, and where you can purchase a North Cape Diploma and have "North Cape" stamped on your postcards. In the afternoon the ship rounds the northernmost tip of Norway. Sometimes a stop is made at GAMVIK where cargo is ferried to the shore by a small boat.

DAY VII

In the early dawn the ship steams into KIRKENES, a barren, windswept town. If you prefer to take only half of the Coastal Steamer voyage, you can fly to Kirkenes, spend the night and then board the ship for the return journey to Bergen. In Kirkenes there is a shore excursion offered which gives you a sample of the countryside as the bus makes its way to the Russian border. The interesting aspect of this trip is the scenery which is surprisingly attractive with trees and farms - more vegetation than one might expect. Leaving Kirkenes, the next stop is at VARDO, the easternmost town in Norway. When the ship docks, walk over to see the 14th-century fortress, now abandoned but with a few rooms open as a museum to the public. The last stop of the day is the old fishing village of BATSFJORD.

DAY VIII

In the morning the ship makes a short stop at the small port of HAVOYSUND and then it is on to HAMMERFEST, renowned as the most northerly town in the world. Hammerfest has been an important commercial center down through the ages because of its protected winter harbor. The town is now new because the Germans burned the old town to the ground in 1944. In the late afternoon the OKSFJORD GLACIER can be seen on the starboard side of the ship. This is Norway's only glacier which comes right down to the sea - a handy item for the fishermen who take their ice directly from the sea "for free". The next stop is SKJERVOY, attractively situated with a backdrop of steep mountains. The final call of the day is TROMSO, which is usually reached about midnight. However, you can still go ashore to watch the freight being loaded and unloaded.

DAY IX

About 9:00 am the ship steams into the HARSTAD port where there is a bus waiting to take the passengers who have made reservations for the overland trip to SORTLAND where they will rejoin the ship. This is a very interesting excursion through the countryside, with a stop to see the charming, very old little stone church at TRONDENES. The bus passes through a fertile valley, then crosses a fjord and continues on to Sortland where the ship usually arrives about the same time as the bus. In the afternoon the ship stops at STOKMARKNES before making its way through the beautiful narrow Raftsund Channel. If time permits, the ship dips into the narrow TROLLFJORD - a very beautiful fjord walled with mountains. Frequently naval ships and yachts will be seen also enjoying the beauty of this especially scenic fjord. There are two more brief stops at SVOLVAER and STAMSUND.

DAY X

In the wee hours of the morning the ship calls at BODO and then later in the morning arrives at ORNES for a brief stop. After breakfast the SVARTISEN GLACIER comes into view. Soon after, you cross the Arctic Circle again before arriving about noon in NESNA, situated on a spit of land between the Sjona and Rana fjords. After leaving Nesna the SEVEN SISTERS (seven granite peaks) come into view. The next stop is BRONNOYSUND, after which the ship detours to the west of Torghatten to view the enormous hole (175 yards long, 115 feet high and 50 feet wide) eroded in the mountain during the Ice Age. The final call of the day is at RORVIK.

DAY XI

The ship arrives back at TRONDHEIM early in the morning, giving time again for sightseeing in this delightful small city. An optional side tour (highly recommended) is to visit the 11th-century NIDAROS CATHEDRAL, the largest medieval building in Scandinavia. A guide explains the history and architecture of this magnificent cathedral where seven kings and three queens have been crowned. Returning to the ship, the bus goes through Trondheim, with views of the river winding through the center of town and Monk Street where many beautiful wooden homes built by the old merchant families remain. The next stop is a brief one about dinner time in KRISTIANSUND and then one more in the early evening at MOLDE.

DAY XII

This is the final day of the cruise and the scenery becomes ever more lovely and verdant as the steamer nears Bergen. The final port of call is at FLORO. More brightly painted cottages and farms dot the shoreline as civilization again draws near. About 2:00 pm the ship steams into Bergen.

Notes: There are 11 ships in the Coastal Fleet, all similar in design. A typical ship, such as the M/S NARVIK, is 4,200 tons, 109 meters long, 16.5 meters wide, carries 410 passengers and has 175 berths on board in various cabin configurations. To give you a general idea of cost, at the time of this guide's publication, the per person price for the roundtrip journey ranged during high season (May 16-August 31) from $1,530 per person for an outside cabin with two lower berths, shower and toilet to $1,005 per person for an inside cabin with upper and lower berth and washbasin. During the off season the rates drop considerably. There are senior citizen rates available for those 67 years and older. Children under three not requiring a special berth travel for 10% of the fare. Children three to twelve travel for 75% of the fare. The five standard shore excursions, offered in summer, can be purchased in advance for about $93.00. If space is available, they can also be purchased on board the ship from the hostess. REMEMBER: Make your reservations early since during peak season, some of the cabins sell out a year in advance.

All rates and special fares are those in effect in January 1987 and are, of course, subject to change.

Reservations for the Norwegian Coastal Voyage can be made through:

BERGEN LINE, INC.
505 Fifth Avenue
New York, N.Y. 10017
tel: (212) 986-2711.

Viking Trails of Denmark

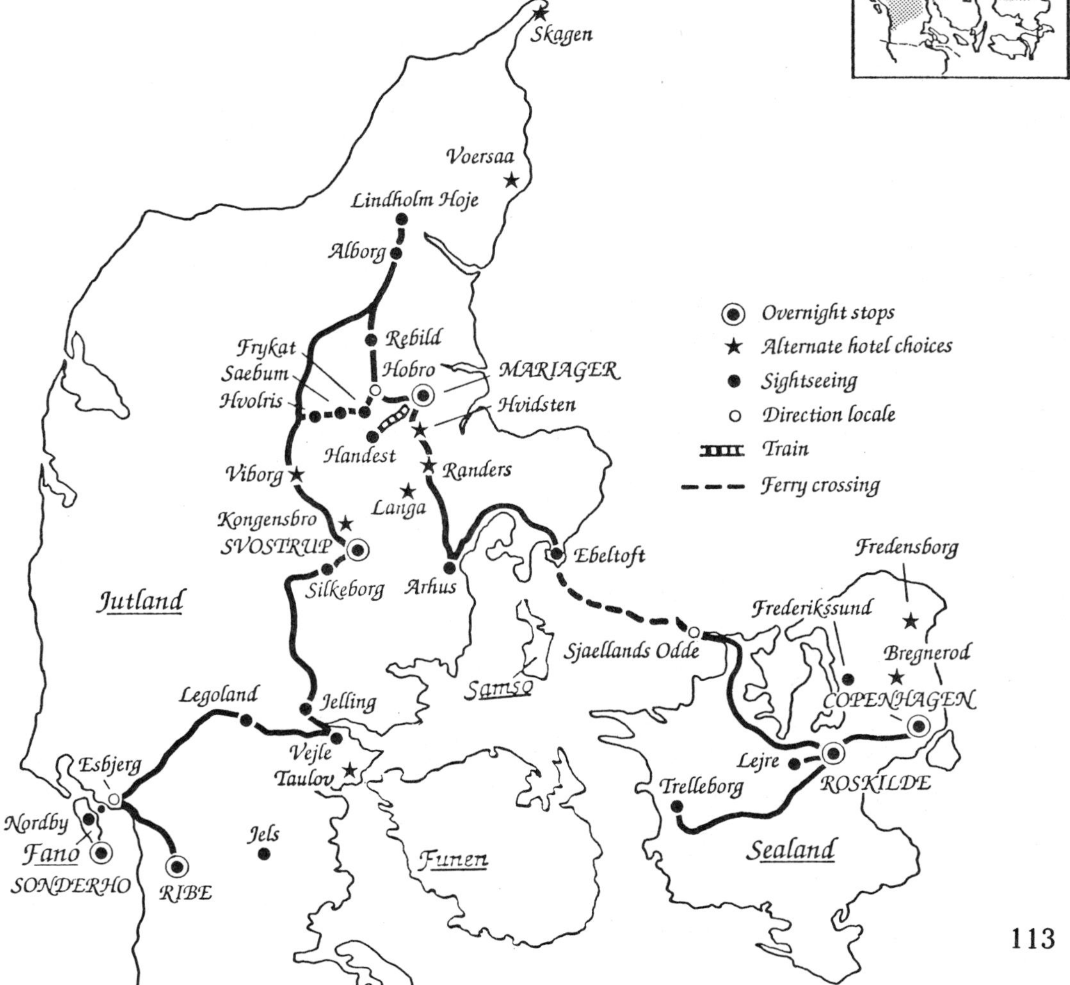

Viking Trails of Denmark

Denmark is a land of lofty dunes, windswept seascapes, vistas stretching out over white crests of wild open seas, protected inlets and sheltered bays. One could not stage a more appropriate setting for the Vikings. There is romance associated with the legends of these people who set out across the ocean in fragile vessels. These canoe-like wooden boats, adorned with intricately carved dragon motifs, were powered by the sheer strenth of men and the leverage of wind and cloth. Much of Denmark's history can be traced back to the days when the Vikings dominated Scandinavia. Many years have passed since the Vikings conquered and ruled Denmark, yet their relics and monuments remain scattered throughout the country and their myths and legends remain a part of Danish culture and heritage. This itinerary follows a trail of Viking discoveries: the fjords, beaches, lakes, moorlands, meadows and villages provide an ideal setting against which to seek out vestiges from the Viking Age.

ORIGINATING CITY COPENHAGEN

"Viking Trails of Denmark" begins in Copenhagen and concludes in South Jutland. However, the itinerary can easily be reversed, making an ideal route from Germany into Denmark and on to Copenhagen. Road numbers have not been specified in the text of this itinerary to avoid confusion as there are numerous roads and freeways from which you can select.

Whichever routing you use, COPENHAGEN makes a perfect beginning or ending for any itinerary. There are many sightseeing possibilities within the city, delightful restaurants and excellent shopping. Beginning on page 44 in the "Highlights of Scandinavia" itinerary are ideas for what to do while in Copenhagen.

DESTINATION I ROSKILDE Svogerslev Kro

When leaving Copenhagen, drive just 30 kilometers west to ROSKILDE. This city has been renowned for centuries because of its beautiful 12th-century CATHEDRAL whose spires dominate the skyline and within whose walls 38 Danish kings and queens are entombed. Since June of 1969 the cathedral's fame has been shared with a fantastic VIKING SHIP MUSEUM. Built to house five Viking ships discovered in Roskilde Fjord, the museum actually opened before restoration of even the first ship was completed so that the public could witness the long, arduous process of fitting the thousands of pieces of wreckage back together to recreate as much as possible of the original skeleton and body of the vessel. It is understood that the ships were sunk in the fairways of Roskilde Fjord with a specific intent to create a blockage and protect this trading town from surprise raids by enemy fleets. Although historians have been unable to associate a particular event with the sinking of the ships, they have determined that it happened at the end of the Viking Age, sometime between 1000 and 1050, a time when Norwegian Vikings ravaged Denmark.

The museum is a vast room whose large glass windows look out to the fjord and fill the museum with natural light, providing a stark but stunning setting for the Viking ships. Their exacting reconstruction is impressive, especially when you consider how long they lay submerged, embedded in the ocean floor, under a mound of stones. When the fragments of wood were brought to the surface they were specially cared for and preserved before any reconstruction could begin.

Each of the ships is a different size and was built for a different purpose. The Deep Sea Trader is a broad solid vessel that either carried settlers from a Norse settlement in Iceland to Denmark or hauled cargo between European countries. Built of pine, oak and lime, the ship measures 16.5 meters in length, 4.5 meters at its widest breadth and was most likely built in southern Norway. It had decks but nowhere for people to take shelter. The Merchant Ship is a trim, oak-built craft, 13.3 meters long and 3.3 meters wide, an example of a typical Baltic cargo vessel. Freight was stowed mid-ship, but again the crew of not more than five or six men were without shelter from the ocean winds and storms. The Warship is long, low and narrow in form, being 18 meters long and 2.6 meters wide. It is very similar to the Ladbyskibet unearthed in Ladby on the island of Funen (page 131). It usually sailed with a crew of 24 men. The Ferry is the smallest of the ships, 12 meters long and 2.5 meters wide, and was fitted for a mast and sail, but, unlike the other boats, it did not have holes for oars. The Longship is about 28 meters in length and was the legendary Viking man-of-war attack vessel. It held a crew of 40 to 50 oarsmen and was constructed from light, resilient oak that afforded it speed and maneuverability.

The museum shows films documenting each stage of the excavation and reconstruction of the ships. There is also a presentation about a group of scouts who built a Viking ship: the vessel was so precisely made, using the same types of tools and methods as the Vikings, that it is considered very important for evaluating the scope and sailing abilities of historic vessels. The Viking Ship Museum is open year round and serves as an impressive exhibition and a most outstanding tribute to the Vikings.

Just southwest of Roskilde is the LEJRE RESEARCH CENTER, an open-air display of reconstructed Iron Age houses and workshops that is open from May to September. To reach the center from Roskilde drive towards RINGSTED, turn right towards HOLBEAK and shortly thereafter turn left towards LEDREBORG and LEJRE. At the Research Center you watch films about Iron Age man and wander through a reconstructed settlement where demonstrations of forging, logging and the use of dugout canoes and horses are given. Character actors live here during the summer months and play the part of Iron Age families. Of further interest, pottery and weaving demonstrations are given.

Note: After leaving Roskilde, this itinerary suggests a routing northwest to catch a ferry to Jutland, but you may detour southwest to TRELLEBORG near Slagelse where a fortified Viking camp has been unearthed and partly reconstructed. The site is open from April to September.

From Lejre return in the direction of Roskilde and just 6 kilometers from the edge of the city, travelling east, you come to SVOGERSLEV and the SVOGERSLEV KRO. This charming thatched inn has been welcoming guests into its cozy restaurant since 1772. The current owner, Mr Flemming Petersen, purchased the inn recently after waiting on its tables for ten years and leasing the building for three. Under his excellent care and instruction, rooms were added to accommodate guests in two separate buildings that exactly match the mood and decor of the original thatched inn. Tucked under the beams of the newly constructed inn are twelve double rooms and one single room, each simply but caringly furnished and all with private bath. The restaurant is the hotel's pride and its kitchen is open daily from 11:00 am to 9:30 pm.

Svogerslev Kro
Roskilde

DESTINATION II MARIAGER Hotel Postgaarden

From Svogerslev follow the signs northwest to NYKOBING and then out to the peninsula's farthest point, SJAELLANDS ODDE. From Sjaellands Odde it is an hour and a half's ferry crossing to Ebeltoft in Jutland. Ferries depart every two hours from 6 am to 10 pm, and while reservations are not needed it is best to call 06 34 1600, Mols-Linien A/S, so that you can coordinate your arrival in Sjaellands Odde with the ferry's departure.

EBELTOFT is a popular vacation spot with holiday houses scattered along its miles of narrow beachfront. The town itself is quite small with a charming main street and a quaint old town hall.

From Ebeltoft the road travels inland, yet still follows the contours of the coastline as it travels south to ARHUS. This is one of Denmark's largest cities and although heavy traffic makes for slow driving it is worth negotiating the busy streets to reach the OLD TOWN, a living museum that stages a 17th- and 18th-century urban environment. A wonderful collection of approximately 60 renovated buildings has been relocated here to stage a town scene including workshops, a cobbler, a post office, a mayor's residence, a customs house, stores and residences. During the summer months costumed actors make the town come alive as they recreate life in the 17th century.

Since you are following the trail of the Vikings, the VIKING MUSEUM in town deserves a visit. Excavations at the Andelsbanken on Clemenstorv during the 1960s revealed remains of a semi-circular rampart with which the Vikings protected their little community of craftsmen, seafarers and merchants 1,000 years ago. The cellar of the Andelsbanken was made into a museum to preserve the reconstructed ramparts. During the last weekend of July the town hosts a Viking Festival at Moesgard Strand.

Approximately an hour's drive north of Arhus, RANDERS (one of Denmark's oldest towns) has also always been an important trade and market center as it is situated where the seaway and 13 roads converge. Like the spokes on a bicycle, the roads radiate from the city and head out into "Jutland's green heart", a region of lush green landscape, magnificent woods, forests, fields and meadows. The old medieval quarter of town has been preserved and is today full of the character and charm of days gone by. The streets and alleys are interesting to wander through and a number of striking half-timbered houses date back to the 15th century. If the month is April, keep a watch on the angles and slopes of rooftops as storks migrate here each year from Egypt to build their rooftop nests.

MARIAGER, to the north of Randers, is a charming village, once known for the roses that used to grow up the facade of most of the buildings. Sadly, however, with the increase of street traffic, the flowers are not as plentiful as they once were. Mariager is also the terminus of a colorful railway line that travels 17 kilometers to the village of HANDEST. Wonderful old locomotives, two steam engines, carriages and goods wagons (dating from 1897, and from 1910 to 1930) are employed to carry passengers along a scenic journey that begins at the bay and travels through forests of beech trees. This beautiful vintage train which runs only in the summer months can be ridden in both directions or one way. The one-way trip takes approximately one hour and schedules begin around 11:00 am, ending around 5:00 pm. You can call (08) 54 18 64, the station in Mariager, for exact departure and arrival times. If you happen to be travelling off-season you can still view the oldest carriage car as it is parked on the tracks of the Mariager Station during the winter months.

Hotel Postgaarden
Mariager

Just opposite the old market place in Mariager is the HOTEL POSTGAARDEN. Behind a wonderful old timbered facade stretching along an uneven cobble-stoned road, this charming inn has almost become the symbol of the town whose citizens rescued it from destruction in 1984. The hotel was restored and Kurt Bjerre elected to manage it. Heavy old beams, original to the house, add character to the cozy rooms. Tea and light snacks are now served at tables covered with brown checked cloths in what is the oldest part of the inn - the

Vicar's Apartment, dating back to 1688. You can settle in any of the four delightful and intimate rooms of the restaurant and enjoy a tasty meal. A corridor bounded by the original 1710 walls leads to the inn's superb bedrooms. Decorated in light wood, all the bedrooms are outfitted with private modern baths and the rooms at the back overlook the herb garden.

DESTINATION III SVOSTRUP Svostrup Kro

Travel a short distance inland, following the banks of Denmark's longest fjord to the town of HOBRO, strategically located at the end of the fjord. Just outside the town a remarkable Viking ring fort, FRYKAT, lies unprotected from the wind, surrounded by farmland. Frykat, probably established under the orders of King Svend Tveskaeg around 1000, is approximately 120 meters in diameter and contained 16 large houses. Next to the grass-covered skeleton of the fortification is a reconstruction of a typical long house. Archaeologists have determined that this was a peaceful community as tools and domestic items such as jewelry were unearthed but no weapons. This Viking settlement substantiates the theory that Hobro was an important Viking port.

Before continuing north it is worth making a detour to the west to SAEBUM where two passage graves have been discovered. Dating back to about 3000 BC, these are considered among the most impressive and best preserved of this Neolithic, new stone age. At HVOLRIS, just a short distance further west of Saebum, on a hillside are archaealogical excavations from the Stone, Bronze and Iron Ages to the Viking period and the Middle Ages. Tombs and exhibitions of unearthed artifacts can be seen and the area explored on foot.

The road from Hobro north to Alborg travels through REBILD NATIONAL PARK. Established 75 years ago by Danish emigrants to the United States, these acres and acres of forested parkland are riddled with hiking trails and on July 4th a celebration of America's independence day takes place that rivals any to be seen in the United States.

ALBORG is the largest city in northern Jutland. Unless you want to explore its shops or sample its restaurants and night life, stay on the ring road as it circles the city and crosses the bridge over the Limfjorden to NORRESUNDBY. Take the first exit after you cross the inlet and follow signs directing you to LINDHOLM HOHE. This site on the outskirts of town is the largest Scandinavian burial site from the Viking period. This windswept hillside with its more than 800 Viking graves is an awesome contrast to the bustling town. The burial sites are surrounded by stone enclosures in the shape of a Viking ship. Viking fields and the remains of a settlement have been uncovered and are detailed and diagramed on billboards.

As you head south to your hotel you will drive through VIBORG, a city that dates back to the 8th century when it was an important trading center and place of pagan sacrifice, later becoming the coronation town for Danish kings. Its CATHEDRAL was founded in 1130 and is one of Denmark's most distinguished granite churches, its towers impressing an image on the city skyline. It is interesting to note that the HAERVEJEN (the ancient military road) that was used by traders, cattle drivers and pilgrims for many centuries passed through this area.

Just north of the lovely city of SILKEBORG, in the small farming village of SVOSTRUP, is the SVOSTRUP KRO, dating from 1834. This inn, tucked behind an arched entry with its own enclosed courtyard, is set on the banks of the Gudena River, a convenient location in the 19th century for welcoming passing bargemen. The inn has nine simply furnished rooms without private bathrooms (there are plans to add ten with bathrooms en suite in the near future) and a charming restaurant. The pub, centrally located in the inn, remains much as it was in the days of the bargemen, filled with conversation and laughter.

Svostrup Kro
Svostrup

DESTINATION IV RIBE Hotel Dagmar

Travel south from Svostrup through the beautiful riverside city of SILKEBORG to JELLING, just outside the city of VEJLE. Although by today's standards Jelling is a small town, it was once the home of Danish kings and queens. In Jelling's churchyard are two great burial mounds, "Gorms hov" and "Thyras hoj", tangible reminders of former times. These are the graves of the Viking King Gorm and his Queen, Thyra, who died about 935. Standing at the front of the church are two stones that are unquestionably the most distinguished written records of ancient time to be found in Scandinavia. One was erected by King Gorm in memory of Queen Thyra and the larger stone was commissioned by their son, Harald Bluetooth, in memory of his parents. Chiselled in granite in ancient script, Gorm's stone is simply inscribed detailing the good his wife did for Denmark. Harald's stone is much more elaborate and calls for remembering his parents, the unification of Denmark, the conquest of Norway and the conversion of Denmark to Christianity. Harald's stone remains on its original site, halfway between his parents' graves.

LEGOLAND, a "Disneyland" built of Lego bricks, is just a few miles west of the city of Vejle, on the outskirts of BILLUND. This is a waist-high exhibition that utilizes over 3,000,000 Lego blocks to make miniature villages, a harbor with model ships, a mini railway, motor boats, an Indian camp, Amalienborg Palace in Copenhagen, Mount Rushmore and the Austrian Alps - to name just a few. Lego was invented by a carpenter, Ole Kirk Christiansen, who began making wooden toys and called them Lego, a play on the Danish words "leg godt", meaning "play well". In 1949 plastic interlocking bricks became part of the Lego collection of toys and by 1955 these had become the trademark of the company and a favorite toy of children the world over. Kirk's son Godtfred decided to create a permanent open-air exhibit of what can be built with Lego blocks. Opened in 1968, the park now includes the Lego world, amusement rides, theaters and restaurants.

RIBE is Denmark's oldest town whose history dates back to ancient times. During the Viking era it was an important trading center and the city continued to thrive on into the Middle Ages. If you are lucky enough to visit Ribe between May 1 and September 15, the enchantment of this delightful town will come to life as you follow the village watchman on his traditional evening rounds and listen to his song and account of the town's dramatic history. His tour starts each evening at 10 pm from Torvet Square onto which the bricked facade of the HOTEL DAGMAR fronts. From the main lobby a stenciled stairway leads to the oldest rooms of the hotel. Found along a creaking, slanting corridor and tucked behind low doorframes, the 18 older rooms are without private bathrooms but have more character than the new wing of modernly appointed rooms. The older front bedrooms look out across the bricked square to the cathedral. Wainscoting and rich tones of gold, green and red decorate the hotel's popular and busy restaurant. The Vaegterkaelderen, the hotel's bar, is a cozy spot for a less formal meal or quiet drink. Breakfast is served in what was once the living room.

Hotel Dagmar
Ribe

DESTINATION V SONDERHO, Fano Island Sonderho Kro

This Viking tour concludes on one of Denmark's most enchanting islands, FANO. To reach the island travel to the coast to ESBJERG, Denmark's largest fishing port, and cross by ferry to NORDBY on Fano. Schedules are limited, but information and reservations can be obtained by contacting the ferry station in Esbjerg at (05) 12 00 00. The passage to the island takes about 20 minutes.

Fano is a captivating island of thatched farmhouses, all detailed with rust and green trim and fronted by beautifully manicured gardens enclosed behind picket fences. A National Trust House, the SONDERHO KRO, an inn ever since it received its license in 1722, is charmingly set against a backdrop of sand dunes. More recently a wing with guestrooms was added. It is built of stucco, painted rust and decked with thatch to match the original inn and the neighboring homes. The bedrooms are individually decorated and named after sailing vessels. This old inn offers excellent food and an extremely inviting atmosphere that is enhanced by low doorways, creaking floors, old clocks and paintings.

Your travel options at the conclusion of this itinerary are many: you can return to the mainland of Jutland and then on to Odense to follow the itinerary "The Fairytale Island of Funen", return to Copenhagen, or continue south into Germany.

Sonderho Kro
Sonderho

There are two Viking festivals that you might want to consider attending if they coincide with your travel times: the first is in Frederikssund, on the island of Sealand, from June to early July and the second is in Jels in South Jutland, from July 1 to 15.

The Fairytale Island of Funen

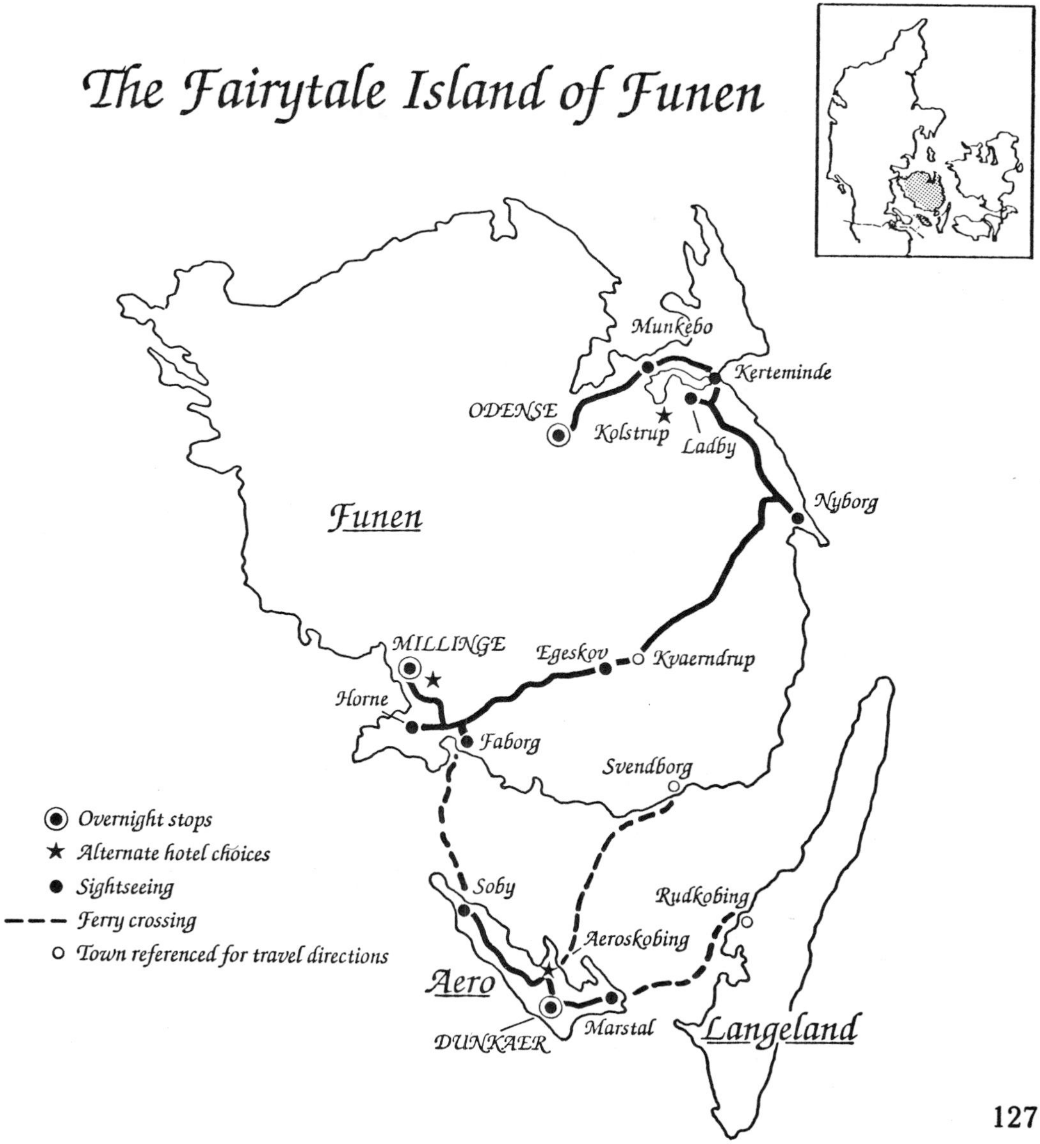

Munkebo
Kerteminde
ODENSE
Kolstrup
Ladby
Nyborg
Funen
MILLINGE
Egeskov
Kvaerndrup
Horne
Faborg
Svendborg
Soby
Rudkobing
Aeroskobing
Aero
Marstal
DUNKAER
Langeland

- Overnight stops
- ★ Alternate hotel choices
- Sightseeing
- Ferry crossing
- Town referenced for travel directions

The Fairytale Island of Funen

Funen is the garden island of Denmark, rich with orchards, hop gardens, fragrant lilacs and billowing fields of wheat. This delightful island nestles between Jutland, to which it is connected by two bridges, and Sealand, linked to Funen by ferry. This is an island to savor for its beauty, history and folklore: its 700 miles of shoreline present grassy dunes stretching down to the water's edge and vistas of silver sand beaches; bustling little ports and industrious harbors are filled with fishing boats, ferries and yachts; villages are found huddled on the slopes of gently rolling hills or snug amongst acres of ever-stretching farmland; passage graves, vessel ruins, castles and manors trace the islanders back to the proud Vikings. The dialect here is said to be spoken by the angels on Sundays: it is also spoken with a keen sense of humor by the warm and friendly islanders.

Aeroskobing
Aero Island

ODENSE, in the center of the island of Funen, was just a small country town when Hans Christian Andersen was born here on April 2nd, 1805. He loved to travel and was quoted as saying, "to travel is to live". Odense, with its maze of narrow cobbled streets which lend character and charm to the city, is a very suitable place to begin this itinerary.

Hans Christian Andersen, whose 156 fairytales are loved by children and adults all over the world, once said he would be the reason that people came to Odense and indeed, for the majority of tourists, his prophecy has come true. Signs all over town direct you to HANS CHRISTIAN ANDERSEN'S HUS, the tiny pastel-washed house where he was born into a poor family, his father a struggling cobbler and his mother a laundress. The family living quarters have been expanded to include a museum about his life, loves (Jenny Lind, an opera singer, was the inspiration for his work "The Nightingale") and works. You can listen in the museum to recordings of several fairytales narrated by Sir Michael Redgrave.

Nearby you can also visit Hans' childhood home, H. C. ANDERSEN'S BARNDOMSHJEM. The house and a narrow wedge of the original cobblestoned street remain sandwiched between department stores and city offices. One small room served as the living room, family shoe workshop and bedroom while the other miniscule room was the kitchen. What is now the tiny museum kiosk was, in Hans' day, home to a family of six. Hans lived in this small abode until he set off for Copenhagen in search of an education and fortune when he was 14 years old.

There are several other very interesting museums in and around Odense. The composer Carl Nielsen's childhood home, BARNDOMSHJEM, has a very interesting exhibit on his childhood. The DANISH RAILWAY MUSEUM houses a collection of historic railway engines, carriages and model trains. The number 2 bus will take you south of town to the spectacular open-air museum, DEN FYNSKE LANDSBY, where 24 rural buildings have been relocated to depict a 17th-century Funen village. There are beautifully furnished thatched, beamed farmhouses, horse stalls, barns, a school, a wind- and watermill, workshops, stores and the Sortebro Inn, where you can dine or enjoy light refreshments. In summer costumed actors and skilled craftsmen recreate life in the 17th century. From mid-July until mid-August Hans Christian Andersen's plays are performed in the adjacent outdoor theater.

Golf Plaza Hotel
Odense

The GOLF PLAZA HOTEL is easy to find on the main road that circles the city, directly across from the east train station. It is just a few minutes' stroll from the town center, Hans Christian Andersen's house, the theater and the pedestrian shopping thoroughfare. This five-story brick facade building with its own pointed turret is suited to the businessman and traveller alike. It has a dramatic lobby with a lovely open rotunda. Most of the bedrooms are furnished in the original formal style while a few others are more contemporary in their decor. The Rosegarden restaurant is exquisitely furnished with handmade leather furniture and is considered to be one of Denmark's finest gourmet restaurants. A bountiful Danish buffet breakfast of rolls, a selection of cold meats, poached eggs, yogurt, juice and coffee is offered in a bright sitting room. One of a group of four hotels, the Golf Plaza is owned by a corporation and although efficiently and caringly managed, do not expect the atmosphere characteristic of an owner-operated inn.

DESTINATION II MILLINGE Falsled Kro

Leave Odense on the 165 in the direction of Kerteminde along the narrow strip of land bounded to the north by the Odense Fjord. About half an hour's drive brings you to MUNKEBO where the MUNKEBO KRO faces an expanse of bay and moored boats. This royal licensed inn serves simple, reasonably priced traditional fare.

In the distance you see the village of KERTEMINDE, a cluster of red-tile roofs stretching along a white sand beach. The gleaming modern harbor and small well-worn boats of the old harbor (Lillestranden) emphasize the important role fishing plays. The heart of the old town is a maze of narrow winding streets.

From Kerteminde continue along the 165 following the bay's southern shore and then turn inland towards Odense and Ullerslev, passing through a cluster of thatched farmhouses to the village of LADBY. Behind the village in a windswept field overlooking the choppy seas of Kerteminde Fjord is the LADBYSKIBET, a museum that contains the ruins of a Viking ship. This ancient site, discovered in 1935, is unusual because it contains the remains of a

Viking chief, his ship, horses, dogs and belongings buried at a time when cremation was considered the standard tradition and practice. The site was discovered by a farmer who sold the parcel to an archaeological team who excavated the ship and its contents. This underground excavation is well worth a visit.

(If you are looking for a luncheon stop, try the ULRIKSHOLM SLOT built in 1636, located farther around the bend of the bay, outside the village of KOLSTRUP. You can see the copper tower and brick frame of the castle in the distance as you drive round the Kerteminde Fjord to the castle's entrance.)

From Ladby retrace your steps toward Kerteminde and then follow the 165 south toward NYBORG. The scenery varies as the road travels along the edge of the coast, passes through forest, is exposed to the crashing surf and then continues inland until it reaches the port city of Nyborg where ferries cross back and forth to Sealand. From 1200 to 1413 Nyborg was the home of the "Danehof", the early Danish parliament. NYBORG CASTLE is especially interesting because it served for centuries as a residence of the kings of Denmark. The oldest ramparts date back to the Romanesque period, about the year 1200. The interior has some fine furniture from the Middle Ages and Renaissance and an interesting collection of weapons. In summer, concerts are held in the Knights' Hall.

Leaving Nyborg, retrace your route on the 165 heading north out of town until it intersects with the 8 which you take in the direction of FABORG. This lovely country road is bounded by expanses of wheat fields, abandoned windmills and an occasional castle. Just outside the town of KVAERNDRUP towers one of Denmark's most regal castles, EGESKOV. Built on wooden pilings in 1554 in the middle of a small lake, the castle is privately owned and at present only occasionally opened to the public although there are plans to have it open on a full-time basis. Visitors come to see the parklike grounds, the gardens and the transport museum filled with carriages, old cars and motorcycles.

Falsled Kro
Millinge

From Egeskov continue along the 8 until it intersects, near Faborg, with the 329 which you follow north to MILLINGE and on to FALSLED and the spectacular FALSLED KRO - the perfect, albeit very expensive, country inn. Nestled in a small farming village, this charming complex of buildings has offered accommodation since the 16th century. The most spectacular lodging is provided in the deluxe suites, recently built in the style of a Funen farmhouse with exposed beams, red tile floors and small paned windows. In the main building make your dinner selection over an aperitif before an inviting log fire. The beamed ceilinged dining room is decorated in soft pink and has masses of pink flower arrangements reflecting in the patina of antique furniture. Most tables enjoy a view through a large arch that opens onto the chef's domain where a massive stove sits center stage and the chef cooks dinner with the help of numerous apprentices and assistants who ensure that every final detail is perfect.

Travel a country road just a few miles southeast of Millinge to the small residential village of HORNE where set on a knoll overlooking the town you find one of Denmark's beautiful circular churches.

A short drive southeast brings you to the old trading port of FABORG with its delightful pedestrian main street bordered by well kept old houses and merchants' homes. There is a lovely pastel-washed church at the heart of town. DEN GAMLE GAARD, an old merchant's house, has been restored, furnished and is open to the public. The town museum is known for its collection of sculptures and paintings by local Funen artists.

You catch a ferry from the harbor for the short boat ride to Soby on AERO ISLAND. The ferry times vary with the seasons, but the ferries begin running around 7:00 am and the last boat leaves around 11:00 pm. Seating and car reservations are strongly recommended due to the popularity of the island and the stream of daily commuters. Reservations can be made once you arrive in Denmark by telephoning (09) 61 14 88 from 8:00 am to 5:00 pm.

You can easily explore Aero Island for it is only 30 miles long and 8 miles wide. While this itinerary suggests travel from Faborg to Soby, other routes docking at Marstal or Aeroskobing would also prove a convenient starting point for touring this jewel of an island.

On this island scattered windmills crest gently rolling hills and acres of farmland stretch down to sandy dunes. Aero's villages are fishing haunts, with AEROSKOBING the most endearing of all. Dating back to the 1680s, the town is a complex of cobblestoned streets that tumble to the harbor. Windows are dressed with lace and soft tones of pink, yellow, blue and cream color the timber-framed buildings that line the narrow streets. The town is famous for its decorated doorways - each individual and extremely artistic in trimmings and detail. The harbor with its collection of brightly painted boats matches the character and charm of the village. Lovely in its simplicity, the town's church dates from 1756. Be sure to visit the town's museums: the AERO MUSEUM on Brogade, HAMMERICH'S HUS with its beautiful display of faience and tiles, and BOTTLE PETER'S MUSEUM where you can admire an array of ships in bottles.

SOBY is a lively small fishing town on a gentle hillside whose winding streets overlook the sea. It has a simple little church and the Skjoldnaes Lighthouse whose warning beacon has directed sailors since 1881.

MARSTAL is a larger, more modern port than Aeroskobing. It is here that ferries dock from Rudkobing on Langeland. The port was famous in the days of tall ships and schooners when there was a large shipbuilding yard here and in the 19th century it was known to shelter as many as 300 sailing vessels. It took local farmers, captains and crews 60 years to build the breakwater by rolling stones from the fields out over the ice and into the water. Ships set sail from here destined for Newfoundland, South America, the United States and England. The delicate spire and illuminated clock of the SEAMEN'S CHURCH marks the town's center. The interior of the church houses a marvelous collection of model ships and displays an unusual black bowl used to christen the town's many illegitimate children. Maritime buffs will also want to visit the JENS HANSEN'S MARITIME MUSEUM on Prinsensgade with its splendid collection of ship models, maritime equipment and treasures brought home by sailors from distant lands.

Plan at least one overnight on Aero Island in order to experience the sight of charming Aeroskobing in the gentle light of morning and to watch the sun set and shade the entire island in a glow of pink. Be warned, however, that in summer months the year-round population of 8,000 soars to 300,000. In June islanders celebrate Midsummer's Eve with huge bonfires and a symbolic burning of the winter's witch astride her broomstick, marking the end of the cold weather.

The island has a limited number of hotels so the DUNKAER KRO in the small farming hamlet of DUNKAER, just 6 kilometers from Aeroskobing, is a central place to stay. Licensed by the king in 1848, this lodging has always been owned by the Clausen family and is today managed by the sixth generation. Accommodation is basic - plain in furnishings and comfort (none of the guestrooms with private bath), but very inexpensive in price and children are extremely welcome. The feeling of a country inn pervades the bustling lounge bar and restaurant: the decor of both is enhanced by a few cherished antiques and charming fabrics.

Dunkaer Kro
Dunkaer

After a visit to Aero you can easily return to the island of Funen and on to Odense or perhaps Copenhagen, via Soby to Faborg, Aeroskobing to Svendborg or to the island of Langeland by ferrying from Marstal to Rudkobing.

Dramatic Castles of Sealand

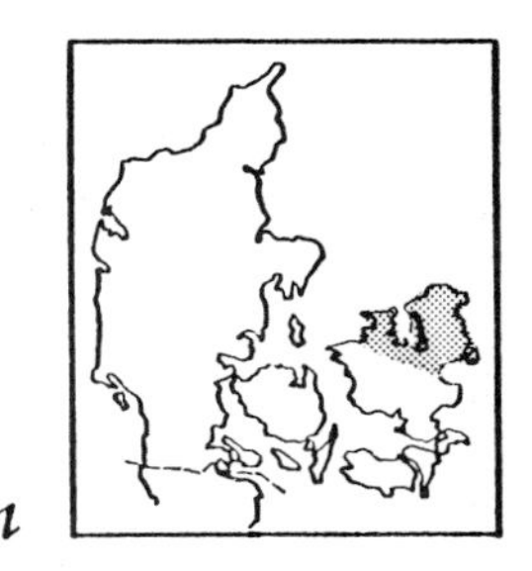

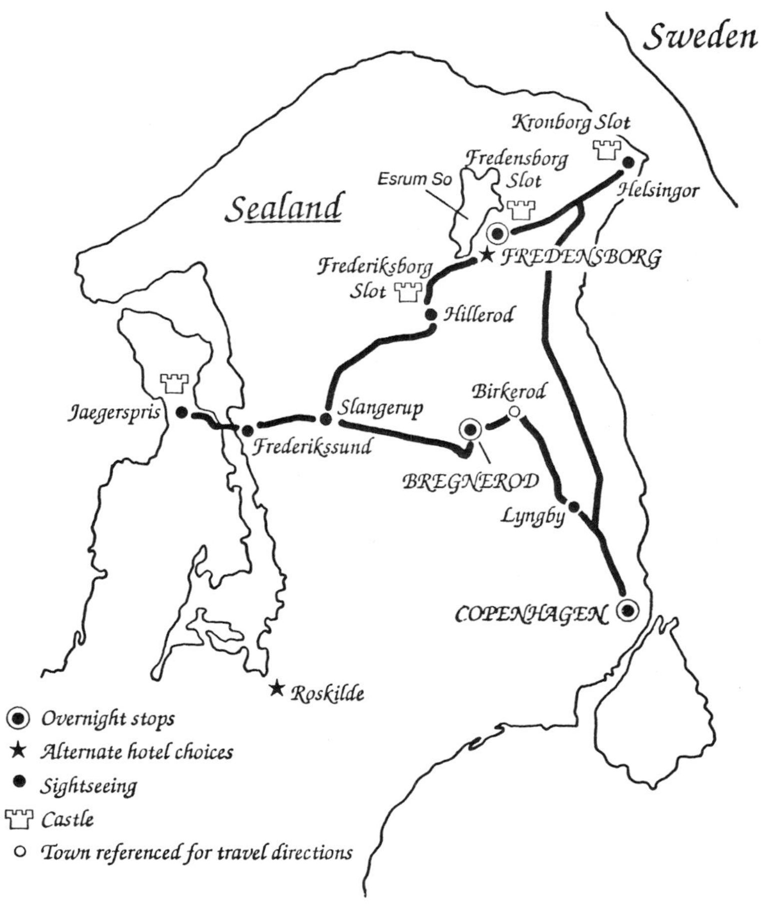

Dramatic Castles of Sealand

Denmark is a small country with over 300 castles, or "slots", scattered across its landscape. Frequently these castles were built for protection and therefore are dramatically positioned looming above a strategic harbor or standing guard on the crest of a hill above a village. At other times it almost seems the castles' purpose is solely decorative as the castles appear on the horizon with a picture-postcard presence, enhancing Denmark's fairytale image. Many of these castles with their regal furnishings, impressive moats, massive towers and splendid museums are open to the public and great fun to visit. Luckily for the traveller, some of Denmark's finest castles are conveniently located for exploring - within a day's journey from Copenhagen. This itinerary makes a loop from Copenhagen, savoring such very special castles as "Hamlet's Castle" at Kronborg and King Christian V's favorite hunting retreat, Jaegerspris Castle.

Kronborg Castle

ORIGINATING CITY COPENHAGEN

COPENHAGEN offers a variety of sightseeing both in the city itself and in the surrounding countryside. Plan your time here according to what most appeals to you before heading north into the countryside. City sightseeing suggestions begin on page 44.

DESTINATION I FREDENSBORG Store Kro

Set at the northeastern tip of Sealand, 45 kilometers along the E4 from Copenhagen, is the old market town of Elisnore or, as the Danes refer to it, HELSINGOR. Positioned across a narrow stretch of water from Swedish soil, the town was recognized as a potentially important stronghold and received its charter in 1426 from the Danish king, Erik of Pomerania. He introduced the greatly opposed "sound dues", a fee to be paid to the Crown by ships desiring passage through the sound. He built Kronborg Castle at the narrowest point of the sound to enforce and assure the collection of dues. Everyday life in the town of Helsingor revolved around the payment of dues, trading with the ships and the warehousing of supplies. Customs officers and shipping agents prospered from the revenue yielded from the dues and built mansions and grand buildings around the town. The overall town plan goes back to the days of Erik of Pomerania and the medieval town center is interesting to explore. Stengade remains as the principal shopping street and runs the length of town down to where the Customs House once stood. In contrast to the rough ways of the visiting seamen, the community of Helsingor appears to have been very pious, with Saint Olai Church and three monasteries: Saint Nicolai Kloster, Saint Anna Kloster (which no longer exists) and the Carmelite Convent.

On a small peninsula overlooking Helsingor's harbor is the impressive KRONBORG CASTLE. This imposing brick fortress, surrounded by a moat, has turrets at its four corners and canons nestled in the surrounding sand dunes. It is referred to as Hamlet's Castle, as it is the setting of William Shakespeare's famous play. The interior of this castle was gutted by a fire in 1629, but the outside walls withstood the flames and the four wings enclosing the courtyard look much as they did in 1585 when Frederik II completed his renovation. He rebuilt Kronborg with a flourish, inspired to enhance its medieval battlements for the benefit of his young bride, his 14-year-old cousin, Sophie. During his reign the castle remained the controlling fortress on the sound. But Frederik II's son saw enemy fleets sail past Kronborg Castle unchallenged and his grandson was to see the conquest of the castle by the Swedes in 1658. Although Christian V built new fortifications on the castle (1670-1699) Kronborg would never be the stronghold it once was. When the sound toll was abolished in 1857, the castle's purpose changed from one of defense to one of regal stature and privilege.

The interior of Kronborg Castle is well worth a tour. The Chapel Royal opens onto the courtyard and is lavish in its fine and intricate detail. The panels on the underside of the gallery are beautiful - interesting as they are similar to the panelled ceilings commissioned by Frederik II for rooms in the royal apartments which were later destroyed. The various wings of the castle house what were once the royal apartments, chambers, meeting rooms, kitchen, ballroom and vast halls and, although sparse in their furnishings, are decorated today with both copies and original tapestries especially designed to cover the castle walls, some old paintings, portraits and a few remaining antiques.

Bastions and connecting underground passageways were ordered built by Frederik II to further strengthen his defensive position. You can tour the dark and damp passages, a portion of which not only served to protect the castle, but also accommodated men, cannons, food supplies and horses. One wide stretch of passageway contains a massive statue of Holger Danske, a slumbering giant, long associated with the castle in a medieval ballad. It is claimed that Holger

Danske will someday awaken and heroically return to rescue Denmark in her hour of need.

Leave Helsingor travelling a short distance southwest along the E4 until it intersects with route 6. FREDENSBORG SLOT is just a short distance from Kronborg Slot in the town of FREDENSBORG, positioned on the shores of Denmark's second largest lake, Lake Esrum. Frederik IV commenced construction of this castle after the conclusion of a 10-year war with Sweden. The crown had owned a farm in the district and the king grew fond of the area when he came here on hunting expeditions. He commissioned his gardener, who had previously been in charge of building royal summerhouses and pavilions, to design this "country house" - a restful environment of both home and garden.

Fredensborg today is the spring and autumn residence of the Royal Family. During the reign of Christian IX, nicknamed "Europe's father-in-law", Fredensborg Slot was a favorite royal base - frequently the gathering place for many of the crowned heads of Europe. Although the extensive forested park and elaborate gardens that surround the palace and extend down to the edge of the lake are an inviting place to stroll and open to the public year round, the castle is open for tours only in July. When the Queen is in residence, the changing of the guard takes place in the courtyard every day at noon. During the summer months, horsedrawn carriages depart from the palace square to tour the grounds: arrangements to hire the carriages can be made at the Asminderod Kro, a historical 17th-century inn.

Directly opposite the entrance to Fredensborg Slot is the STORE KRO, which King Frederik IV had built to accommodate his guests. The public rooms are filled with antique furniture and the spacious dining room is renowned for its cuisine. There are 22 traditionally furnished bedrooms in the main building, with more rooms in an annex across the street. Because of its history and close proximity to the palace, this is a popular hotel, and, although open year round, accommodation is expensive and difficult to secure during the summer months.

Store Kro
Fredensborg

DESTINATION II   BREGNEROD   Bregnerod Kro

On the outskirts of HILLEROD, just a short distance along route 6 from Fredensborg, is FREDERIKSBORG SLOT. Hillerod is a beautifully situated town that has grown up around its dramatic castle just south of the Grib Skov Forest. The castle is named for King Frederik II who acquired the Manor of Hillerodsholm from the Danish naval hero Herluf Trolle in 1560. It was actually an exchange of properties dictated by the king and he had the following verse inscribed on the walls to commemorate his feat:

"Frederik the Second of pious renown,
An exchange hath made His Grace:
Hillerodsholm passed to the Crown,
Skovkloste did Herluf's replace.
1560
Frederiksborg is now my name,
Thus Frederik me did call.
Both far and wide hath spread his fame,
Exceeding lords and princes all."

However, what exists today - a dramatic castle rising out of a little island surrounded by water - was built by his son, King Christian IV. As a young man, Christian developed a fondness for this idyllic setting and decided to level the original buildings and commission a new castle designed in the more lavish Renaissance style. Frederiksborg became his elaborate home where he entertained and impressed guests. From its statued frescoes on the outside to intricate detailing on the inside, Frederiksborg Castle remains one of the most beautiful pieces of architecture in Scandinavia. The ornate castle chapel is exquisite and it was here, throughout the period of absolute monarchy (1660-1848), that coronations were held. It remains today as the chapel of the Danish Orders of Chivalry.

In 1859 a fire destroyed most of the interior of the castle. Funds contributed by the Royal Family, the Treasury and private individuals served to repair the roof and only some of the apartments. In 1877 J. C. Jacobsen, the founder of Carlsberg Breweries, took a special interest in the castle and submitted a plan to restore it to its original splendor. He masterminded a business scheme to establish the castle as a national historical museum and finance it as a separate department of the Carlsberg Foundation. The museum was completed in 1884 and remains today an independent department of the Carlsberg Foundation: profits from the brewery contribute to its upkeep. Because of Mr Jacobsen's gift, people from all over the world can enjoy the splendor of Frederiksborg

Castle and the extensive collection of paintings, portraits, furniture and art housed within its walls. With a printed sheet in hand describing the various rooms, you can tour the castle without a guide, at your own pace.

Continue southwest from Hillerod along the 6 to SLANGERUP and then follow the 53/207 to FREDERIKSSUND which is known for its Viking festival held here each year in late June and early July. The town sits across the Roskilde Fjord from JAEGERSPRIS which means "Hunter's Delight". This royal hunting lodge dates back six centuries, its size and shape changing over the years as successive owners have added and altered. The surrounding parkland is lovely: a dense forest of giant oak trees interspersed with moors, lakes and open meadows. When absolute monarchy was abolished, Jaegerspris passed to the state.

However, in 1854 Frederik VII bought Jaegerspris from the state with his own funds for use as a private residence. Much to the disapproval of the public, the king had married an actress, Countess Danner, with a "scarred" past - she had a child out of wedlock by a baron. Jaegerspris became their private retreat, an escape from the harsh gossip in Copenhagen. When the king died, the house became his widow's and she started an orphanage for girls and trained them to be servants: it is interesting to learn that at one time as many as 400 girls resided here. Part of the castle today remains a home for orphans. Although Frederik VII is buried in the Roskilde Cathedral, Countess Danner is buried on the grounds of Jaegerspris, which, before her death, she bequeathed to the nation as a museum, funded by a private foundation of her husband's. She decreed that it remain furnished as it was in her time. A tour of the house takes you through the entrance hall, reception room, study and Countess Danner's sitting room.

Retrace your path along route 207, east, in the direction of Slangerup and FARUM. Just outside Farum to the north is a delightful thatched inn, the BREGNEROD KRO, which has existed as a restaurant for almost 200 years. The menu offers a large selection of regional specialties, from stuffed filet of plaice with creamed shrimps to a luncheon platter of herring, pickled salmon, tenderloin of beef and Brie cheese. An attractive wing of nine bedrooms has been built to accommodate overnight guests.

Bregnerod Kro
Bregnerod

DESTINATION III COPENHAGEN

Bregnerod lies just 25 kilometers north of Copenhagen. However, allow enough time on your return to Denmark's capital city to visit FRILANDSMUSEET, an open-air museum in LYNGBY. To get there from the Bregnerod Kro, travel a small, unmarked country road in the direction of BIRKEROD, and, when there, head south on route 19 to Lyngby.

Denmark has a number of open-air museums, but the Frilandsmuseet at Lyngby is definitely the most outstanding. An assortment of buildings that date back 200 years - farmhouses, a school, a hospital, stores, craftshops, wind- and watermills and country homes from all over Denmark - have been restored and transplanted to this site. Both the exteriors and interiors of the buildings are detailed and furnished appropriately for their era. Wandering through the complex creates a vivid and lasting impression of life in the Danish countryside two centuries ago. In summer the community comes alive with folk dancing, costumed townspeople and skilled craftsmen. Located just 10 kilometers outside the city limits, the Frilandsmuseet is a wonderful destination and worth spending the day exploring before you drive to Copenhagen.

Finland Fantasy

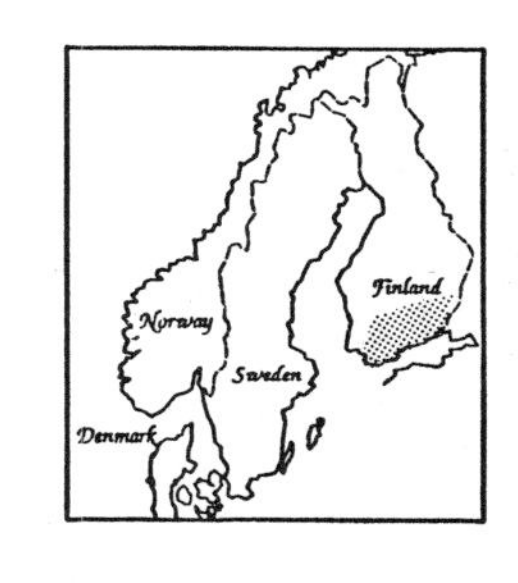

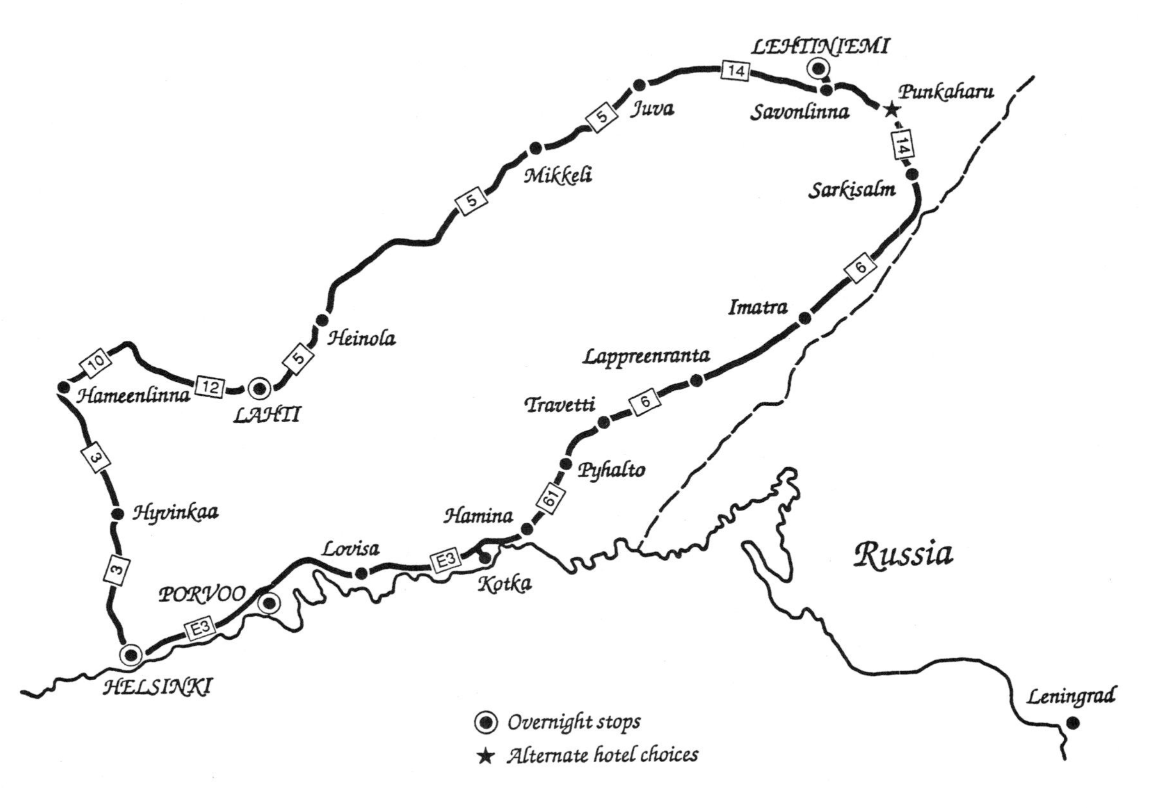

Finland Fantasy

Finland is a treasure chest of beauty ... yet few tourists ever venture farther than Helsinki. Fortunately, you can easily savor some of Finland's most splendid landscapes by renting a car in Helsinki and making a leisurely loop through the countryside. Finland is called "The Land of Thousands of Lakes", which is an understatement: 187,888 lakes have been counted - there are probably even more. Most are located in the southeastern portion of the country, making this area of the map look like a lace doily, with bodies of water separated by threads of land creating an intricate pattern. Sometimes the islands are just toy-like dots of land with a few trees, seeming to float on the water. This itinerary takes you into the lake district: first visiting the picturesque coastal village of Porvoo (whose colorfully painted wooden houses date back to the 16th century), then almost bumping into the Russian border at Imatra (famous for its waterfalls), then crossing the Punkaharau Ridge (which threads its way across the lakes), then visiting the 15th-century city of Savonlinna (with its dramatic lake castle), then visiting Lahti (one of Finland's ski centers) before returning to Helsinki.

Olavinlinna Fortress
Savonlinna

Finland is really not a "country inn" country. It took a great deal of research to be able to offer you hotels with character, and those included in this book are usually very simply decorated. (However, even the simplest of hotels in Finland has tucked away within it the basic necessity of life - the sauna - where you can rejuvenate your mind and body after a day of sightseeing.) If you are uncomfortable staying at unsophisticated hotels, then make your headquarters in Helsinki and take daytrips into the countryside. But, if you like the idea of sleeping in an ornate Victorian mansion built by a Russian general and an 18th-century country manor with its own sauna by the lake, then rent a car and come along. Finland's charm does not lie in the quality of her hotels but in her countryside's serene, unspoiled beauty.

ORIGINATING CITY HELSINKI

Almost all tourists to Finland begin their trip in HELSINKI: and well they might, since it is a fascinating old city. The location which attracted the first settlers is still superb. The beautiful harbor is fringed with romantic little islands - some tiny, some large, all beautiful. If possible, try to arrive by one of the giant ferries which inch their way into the harbor. This is the romantic approach to this colorful city whose cheerful market place is adjacent to the dock.

If you are arriving by boat, the PALACE HOTEL on the harbor is a convenient place to stay - the Viking Line from Stockholm pulls up to the dock almost across the street from the hotel. The Palace Hotel is modern and has no structural charm, but the view from the rooms facing the harbor is spectacular. If you are arriving by train and prefer hotels with more olde-worlde charm, the SEURAHUONE SOCIS, near the train station, is an excellent choice.

Helsinki offers a colorful palette of choices for sightseeing both in the city and in the countryside. Suggestions on what to see and do begin on page 37.

DESTINATION I PORVOO Haikko Manor Hotel

No need to be up at the crack of dawn today as your destination tonight, PORVOO, lies only 48 kilometers east of Helsinki. The road to Porvoo is well signposted but, before reaching the town, watch carefully for a sign marking a road to the right to the HAIKKO MANOR HOTEL - your home for the night. As you leave the highway, signs will continue to direct you to the hotel which is located on an inlet of the sea.

Haikko Manor Hotel
Porvoo

The present hotel dates from the turn of the century, but the history of the manor dates back to the 14th century when a Dominican monastery occupied the site. When making reservations be sure to request the main building because, adjacent to the original inn, a large conference center has been constructed which is starkly modern and has no charm. The main building has only a few guestrooms, none outstanding in decor, but all pleasant in a frumpy sort of way and those with a view out to the water are particularly nice. The public rooms are old-fashioned in mood with many Victorian pieces of furniture.

After checking into the hotel, ask for directions to Porvoo, about a 15-minute drive farther on. As you approach the town there are rather unattractive apartment buildings and factories, but when you reach the river the "real" Porvoo comes into view, with its row of colorful wooden houses reflecting in the river. Cross the bridge, find a place to park your car and then continue to explore on foot. You will need comfortable shoes because this quaint village consists of small cobbled lanes which climb the hill from the river. Porvoo, one of Finland's oldest towns (dating from the 14th century) has many of its wonderful old buildings still intact, making this one of the most picturesque towns in Finland.

DESTINATION II SAVONLINNA-LEHTINIEMI Hotel Rauhalinna

When you leave the Haikko Manor Hotel continue east from Porvoo through the town of LOVISA where, if you look carefully, you see remains of the old town walls. Leaving Lovisa, follow signs for KOTKA along the main highway and on to a motorway. Just as you get on the motorway watch for your exit for LANGINKOSKI RAPIDS, where Czar Alexander III built his imperial fishing lodge, a visit to which is most worthwhile. The living quarters in the lodge are rustic in a "kingly" sort of way. Although this is a simple log construction, the interior (which is now a museum) has displays of splendid dinnerware and the finest of embroidered linens. Portraits hang on the wall of the czar and his beautiful Danish wife who loved to holiday here in their rustic hideaway.

Return to the motorway and drive northeast to HAIMINA, the center of which was laid out in 1722 in a most unusual circular pattern. Some of the walls from fortifications still stand. Park in the center of town and wander around the central square amongst the old buildings.

From Haimina, leave the coastal highway and head northeast through PYHALTO and TRAVETTI for LAPPEENRANTA, where it is worth a stop to see in the central plaza Finland's oldest ORTHODOX CHURCH. A few minutes' drive from the church, on a low plateau, is a park with ruins of an old fortress.

From Lappeenranta it is only about 17 kilometers to IMATRA, an industrial town famous for its rapids which are channeled for power. The rapids are released every Sunday in the summer as a tourist attraction.

From Imatra continue north on the 6 to SARKISALMI where the road divides. Here you leave 6 and continue northwest on the 14 heading toward Savonlinna. In a few minutes you will fnd yourself driving through one of the most scenic areas in Finland - a parklike oasis of gentle lakes and quiet forests. More and more lakes appear until the road becomes almost a bridge of land threading its way through a maze of little islands. This natural causeway, called the PUNKAHARJU RIDGE, stretches for 7 kilometers through this area of great natural beauty. If it is mealtime and you would like an excuse to linger in this lovely lakeland, watch for signs to the left of the road to the VALTION HOTEL in Punkaharju. This small hotel, sheltered in a forest overlooking the lake, is Finland's oldest inn. It was built in the 19th century by the Czar as a gamekeeper's lodge and today still maintains a delightful Victorian ambiance with a wooden facade enhanced with fancy gables and carved curlicues. The hotel serves simple meals in a porchlike dining room whose large windows open to a view of the lake.

From Punkaharju it is about 35 kilometers until (just before reaching Savonlinna) you take a road to the right heading north to LEHTINIEMI. Watch the signs very carefully because, although Lehtiniemi is only 16 kilometers from Savonlinna, the roads are small and the HOTEL RAUHALINNA a bit tricky to find. When you get close, you will be able to spot the hotel on a knoll above the lake, with a lawn stetching down to the water. You will recognize the hotel immediately because it is quite an intriguing creation - a gingerbread fantasy of turrets, cupolas, balconies and lacy wood carving.

Hotel Rauhalinna
Savonlinna

This villa was built at the end of the 19th century by an officer in the czar's Royal Army, General Weckman, as a romantic hideaway for his wife. Inside the decor is rather stilted, with fancy antiques combined with uninteresting modern furniture. However, the detail work of the interior is fabulous, with carved doors, ornate columns, charming tiled stoves, elaborate chandeliers, parquet floors and fanciful ceilings. There are a few old pieces of furniture in the bedrooms but most are quite plain. The hotel is especially popular in summer when visitors arrive by boat from Savonlinna to dine. This is a romantic hotel, but not suitable for those who want perfect decor.

The surrounding area has several interesting sights, so, after settling into the hotel, drive back to the main highway, following the signs to SAVONLINNA. As you drive into town, you will soon see on your left Finland's finest castle, OLAVINLINNA FORTRESS, a dramatic stone fortification dominating a small rocky island in the lake. Park your car and walk over the footbridge to the fortress. The tours are excellent but "real" castle lovers will be saddened as the interior has been completely reconstructed. In the spacious courtyard a popular Opera Festival is held during July and several other concerts and theatrical presentations are staged here during the rest of the year.

In KERIMAKI, 23 kilometers east of Savonlinna, there is an interesting church dating from 1840 which should not be missed. This church, which holds 5,000 people, is reputed to be the largest wooden church in the world. It was built by a local man who emigrated to America and made his fortune. The story goes that the enormous size of the church is due to the builders' interpreting feet as meters.

In summer, when the weather is fine, the Savonlinna area is a perfect base for exploring SAIMAA LAKE. Many colorful, spunky little boats depart from the harbor in Savonlinna heading out in every direction. The lakes are connected by canals offering a wonderful opportunity to explore this beautiful area by boat.

DESTINATION III LAHTI Mukkula Manor House Hotel

From Savonlinna, continue west for the 100-kilometer drive to MIKKELI, where there are several interesting buildings to see, including a lovely rural wooden parish church dating from the first part of the 19th century and government offices from 1843. There is also a display called MINILAND, a miniature village of buildings built on the tiny scale of 1 to 20. From Mikkeli, continue southwest on the 5 through HEINOLA and on to LAHTI.

As you approach the outskirts of Lahti, watch for a road branching off to the right toward the MUKKULA MANOR HOUSE HOTEL which is located within the Lahti city park that stretches along the eastern shore of Lake Vesijarvi, only a short drive from the center of town. As the road winds into the park you cannot miss the Mukkula Manor House Hotel, a mustard-yellow wooden building accented with white trim. This 18th-century manor house has been recently refurbished and is now one of the most pleasant small inns in Finland. The reception area and dining room have a smattering of antiques and the bedrooms are extremely bright and airy with an attractive country flair.

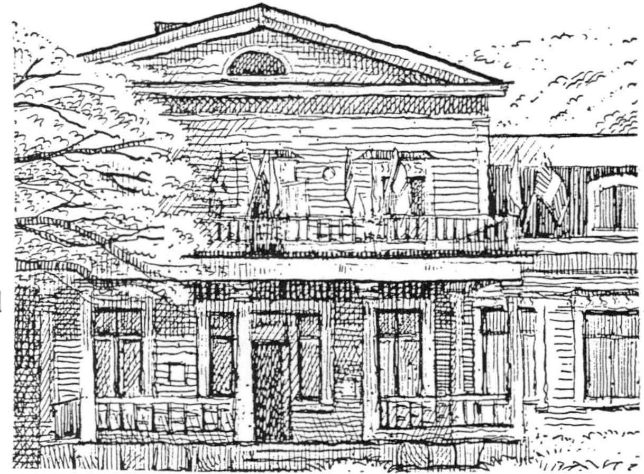

Mukkula Manor House Hotel
Lahti

You will certainly want to do some sightseeing while in Lahti. The downtown area is attractive, mostly modern, but with a few older buildings - the new town hall, designed by Saarinen in 1912, blends beautifully with a wooden church built in 1890. On Sundays in the summer there is a quaint, colorful train, the PIKKU-JUMPO STEAM LOCOMOTIVE, which chugs the 35 kilometers north from Lahti to Heinola. A fun outing is to take the train to Heinola and then return to Lahti through the canals on an old-fashioned little boat, the M/S AINO.

On the eastern edge of town is an enormous sports facility. Lahti is one of the winter sports centers for Finland and within this park is a fabulous assortment of sporting facilities: several giant ski jumps, a sports arena, olympic pool, etc.

If you have children with you they will enjoy visiting the nearby MESSILA HOLIDAY CENTER where there are various carnival-type rides. Adults too will enjoy a visit here to browse through the handicraft and shopping arcade.

Continuing west from Messila, you will come in a few minutes to a large villa on the left-hand side of the road which is now an art gallery open to the public. A 16-kilometer drive farther brings you to HOLLOLA where there is an exquisite 14th-century wooden church.

DESTINATION IV HELSINKI

Rather than taking the direct route to Helsinki (100 kilometers on the E8), sightsee en route by heading west on the 12 for about 48 kilometers, then taking the 10 south to HAMEENLINNA to visit HAME CASTLE, a 13th-century fortress with moats, ramparts and a small museum. Jean Sibelius, the famous composer, was born in Hameenlinna in 1865 and his childhood home is now open to the public.

From Hameenlinna, it is about 105 kilometers to Helsinki. Stop en route at HYVINKAA. Here railway buffs will enjoy a visit to the RAILWAY MUSEUM where among the many attractions are two of the czar's imperial coaches. From Hyvinkaa, it is an easy hour's journey back to Helsinki. If your holiday in Finland is over and you are flying to your next destination, the highway into Helsinki will take you conveniently near the airport.

Map of Denmark Showing Hotel Locations

Aeroskobing is a charming port village of cobbled streets lined by pastel-washed buildings with decorative front doors. Set back off one of Aeroskobing's main streets, facing onto its own inner courtyard, is the conveniently located Hotel Aerohus. The building, dating back to 1785, was converted to a hotel in 1936 by its owner, Johan Phillip Bonsack, whose name is inscribed above the hotel entry. It was purchased in 1954 by the Christensen family who have concentrated on restoring the Aerohus, building by building, ever since. The Christensens and their longtime staff try - and succeed - in creating a homey atmosphere in this family-run hotel, serving especially good homemade food. The bedrooms are found either in the sienna red main building or in an annex tucked off at the back. The furnishings are a little too modern in style for my taste, but the location and friendly service cannot be surpassed, while the large gardens and quiet surroundings provide a most restful setting. The island of Aero lies an hour's ferry ride away from the main island of Funen. Although ferry service is frequent, car and passenger reservations are strongly recommended and can be made by telephoning (09) 52 10 18.

HOTEL AEROHUS
Owners: Birthe and Svend Christensen
Vestergade 38
5970 Aeroskobing
Aero, Denmark
tel: (09) 52 10 03
35 Rooms - DKK 370
Closed: Dec 29 to Jan 20
Credit cards: None
Charming village
Located S of Funen, on Aero island

This is a delightful thatched inn set on a country road just half an hour's drive from Copenhagen, its location convenient to both the capital city and some of Denmark's most remarkable castles. Freddie Jacobsen, who bought the inn in 1974 after having worked there for a number of years as a waiter, is your host. He extends a gracious, warm, welcoming smile and is present to see that service and attention to detail remain excellent and personal. The Bregnerod Kro has existed as a restaurant for almost 200 years. The menu offers a large selection of regional specialties, from stuffed filet of plaice with creamed shrimps to a luncheon platter of herring, pickled salmon, tenderloin of beef and Brie cheese. An attractive wing of nine bedrooms has been built to accommodate overnight guests. These are tastefully decorated, with light oak furniture, cream walls, dark beams, rust highlights on door trims, bright airy print fabrics and fresh flower arrangements, and all are equipped with a mini bar and television. Room 9 is a large corner apartment that looks out the back onto an expanse of woods and parkland. A delicious, hearty, country breakfast of Danish pastries, boiled eggs, meats and crusty rolls is served in the same wing as the bedrooms.

BREGNEROD KRO
Owner: Freddie Jacobsen
Bregnerod, 3520 Farum
(Sealand) Denmark
tel: (02) 95 00 57
9 Rooms - DKK 560
Open: All year
Credit cards: All major
Thatched inn
Located 25 km N of Copenhagen,
3 km outside Farum

The Hotel D'Angleterre, an elegant, traditional hotel on Kongens Nytorv (the King's New Square) is conveniently located not far from the waterfront, the maze of downtown shops, the Royal Palace and the Royal Theater (opposite the hotel). This is not a small hotel but rather sophisticated, expensive and large, with all the services and luxuries to match. Inside, the decor is that of a grand European hotel, with a spacious marble lobby, a bar panelled with rosewood and groups of leather chairs which give an English gentlemen's club atmosphere. La Reine Pedanque is an exceptional gourmet restaurant, while the glass-domed Palm Court, once the carriageway, is a favorite gathering place for lunch and afternoon tea. A grand sweeping staircase leads you upstairs to the bedrooms which are spacious and well equipped with a mini bar, television, video and large bathroom. There are 17 suites, the most famous of which is the Royal Suite, whose sitting room is large enough for a cabinet meeting. Built as a manor house in 1594, the Angleterre became a hotel in 1795 and remained so until World War II when it served as the headquarters of the German occupation forces.

HOTEL D'ANGLETERRE
Manager: Per Kjellstrom
Kongens Nytorv 34
1050 Copenhagen, (Sealand) Denmark
tel: (01) 12 00 95 telex: 15877
139 Rooms - DKK 1575
Open: All year
Credit cards: All major
U.S. Rep: Leading Hotels of the World
Rep tel: 800-223-6800
Elegant, olde-worlde hotel
Located centrally, near the old port

I was delighted to happen upon this hotel and thought it was a true "discovery" until I found it is represented worldwide by Best Western. With just 66 rooms, 10 of which are suites with individual kitchenettes, this is a small city hotel, facing onto a relatively quiet street, whose white facade is shaded by trees. Inside a personal air prevails and the management fulfills their promise of assuring each guest's comfort. Mrs Bente Noyons is often present in the hotel, striving to improve upon yesterday's goals. Just off the entry, on either side, are quiet, very homey sitting areas. From the entrance hall a doorway leads to a peaceful inner courtyard which on warm days is a haven for a quiet place to write cards and enjoy a drink or pot of tea. On the second floor is a bright and airy breakfast room where drinks are available throughout the day. The bedrooms are lovely, thoughtful in decor, and all with private bath. The suites, compared to similar rooms in larger, more expensive hotels, are a true bargain. This is a lovely place to stay where you will receive personal attention and care as if you were a guest in Mrs Noyons' home.

HOTEL NEPTUN
Owner: Bente Noyons
Skt. Annae Plads 18
1250 Copenhagen, (Sealand) Denmark
tel: (01) 13 89 00 telex: 19554
66 Rooms - DKK 1040
Open: All year
Credit cards: All major
U.S. Rep: Best Western
Rep tel: 800-528-1234
Personalized service, no restaurant
Located in the center of Copenhagen

Weathered buildings lean together and cafe tables cluster on the sidewalk to line the waterfront of this colorful and charming district of old Copenhagen. The 71 Nyhavn Hotel lies in a converted warehouse at the end of the docks opposite the hydrofoil boats that depart for Malmo, Sweden, and next to the ferryboats for Oslo, Norway. The location is perfect: just a short walk to the Royal Palace, the Royal Opera and the famous shopping street, Stroget; or, it is just a nice stroll to view the Mermaid. If you don't want to leave your room, you can look out at the water traffic and the towers of the city through small windows set into the hotel's thick walls. Heavy old beams have been retained throughout and tremendously enhance the decor. Be warned that the standard rooms can be a bit small but the six corner suites are lovely and worth the extra expense. For dining the hotel has two superb restaurants: the Pakhuskaelderen is in the warehouse and specializes in refined Danish-French cuisine; docked quayside is the Fyrskib, one of the last Danish lightships, converted into a fish restaurant.

71 NYHAVN HOTEL
Owner: A. Arp-Hansen
Manager: Bente Hjorth
Nyhavn 71, 1051 Copenhagen
(Sealand) Denmark
tel: (01) 11 85 85 telex: 27558
82 Rooms - DKK 1348
Open: All year
Credit cards: All major
U.S. Rep: American Wolfe International
Rep tel: 800-223-5695
In a converted warehouse
Located on the old waterfront of Copenhagen

Sitting directly across from Copenhagen's train station, near Tivoli Gardens, The Plaza Hotel enjoys a wonderful location. Since its opening in 1914 it has set for itself a high standard of excellence and over the years has been considered as "the" place to meet, being very popular with a sophisticated "in" crowd. Privately owned and managed until as recently as 1982, The Plaza prides itself on personalized service. Wood-panelled walls bring a traditional elegance to the handsome lobby where the soft ticking of an antique grandfather clock welcomes you. Settle into the hotel's famous Library Bar whose walls boast a rich display of leather bound books and oil paintings and whose dramatic, domed, stained glass ceiling is most impressive. The Baron of Beef is a restaurant recognized as one of Denmark's finest and the Flora Danica creates a lovely environment in which to sample fine Danish cuisine. A beautiful, bevelled glass elevator travels the six floors up to the hotel's handsome bedrooms and suites, all of which have been recently renovated. The sixth-floor rooms are tucked under beams and were at one time servants' quarters.

THE PLAZA HOTEL
Manager: Sophie Weibull
Bernstorffsgade 4
1577 Copenhagen, (Sealand) Denmark
tel: (01) 14 92 62 telex: 15330
98 Rooms - DKK 1495
Open: All year
Credit cards: All major
U.S. Rep: Leading Hotels of the World
Rep tel: 800-223-6800
Intimate olde-worlde hotel
Located adjacent to the train station

The island of Aero is a distance of one hour's travel time by ferry from the coastal town of Svendborg. The Dunkaer Kro is a hotel sitting in the middle of this idyllic island, located just 4 kilometers from the quaint, picturesque port town of Aeroskobing. Licensed by the king in 1848, this simple inn has always been owned by the Clausens and is managed to date by the sixth generation of their family. The accommodation is basic and plain in furnishings and comfort (no room has a private bathroom), but is very inexpensive and children are extremely welcome. The feeling of a country inn pervades the lounge bar and restaurant: the decor of both is enhanced by a few cherished antiques and charming fabrics. The Dunkaer Kro is described by the owner as a "typical" Danish village inn, known for a very tasty meal with ample portions - a nice place to bring children. In the summer months guests dine in the garden and, year-round, at night the laughter of the local clientel, perched on stools at the bar, wafts through the halls. Although the English spoken by the management is limited, you are made to feel very welcome by the Clausens.

DUNKAER KRO
Owner: Ejvind Clausen
Dunkaervej 1
5970 Aeroskobing
Aero, Denmark
tel: (09) 52 15 54
7 Rooms - DKK 275
Open: All year
Credit cards: None
Inexpensive inn
Located S of Funen, on the island of Aero

Located north of Copenhagen, about 2 kilometers from Fredensborg Palace, the Pension Bondehuset is reminiscent of an inviting English bed and breakfast. Dating back over 180 years, the inn's thatched buildings nestle under trees set on 3 private acres of parkland whose sandy paths lead the short distance down to the shores of beautiful Lake Esrom. Karin Larsen, the Bondehuset's delightful hostess, offers accommodation for a rate inclusive of breakfast and dinner. Served around six, the delicious dinner includes soup or salad, a main entree, dessert and coffee. Wine and beer are available for an additional charge. Delightful views of Lake Esrom can be enjoyed from the dining hall as well as from the adjoining, tastefully decorated drawing rooms where one is welcome to linger either before or after dinner. In warm weather tables are set outside the restaurant on a delightful patio. Recently remodeled, the bedrooms are found in a neighboring building and are simple but sweet in their decor. Room 20 is the largest, a corner double that faces onto the water and enjoys the luxury of its own sitting area. Room 18, also a double room, looks out to the lake.

PENSION BONDEHUSET
Owner: Karin Juel Larsen
Sorup, 3480 Fredensborg
(Sealand) Denmark
tel: (02) 28 01 12
15 Rooms - * DKK 415
* Rate includes dinner
Open: Apr 1 to Oct 15
Credit cards: None
Lakeside setting
Located 50 km N of Copenhagen

In contrast to the homey appeal of the Pension Bondehuset, the Store Kro is a more formal hotel, located directly opposite the gates to Fredensborg Palace, and frequently caters to touring groups. The inn was built in 1723 by King Frederik IV to accommodate royal guests. Margit and Erik Brandt, the new owners, are renowned designers and they have supervised the total redecoration of the hotel which is full of antiques and has a spacious restaurant dramatically decorated with murals. The main building, which has had to be rebuilt twice because of fire damage, houses 22 traditionally furnished bedrooms. The balance of the bedrooms are found in an annex across the street - the annex is actually the original inn. Because of its history and close proximity to the palace, this is a popular hotel, and, although open year round, accommodation is expensive and difficult to obtain during the summer months.

STORE KRO
Owner: Erik Rud Brandt
Managers: Henrik Walbom, Rudi Bugsgang
Slotsgade 1 & 6
3480 Fredensborg, (Sealand) Denmark
tel: (02) 28 00 47 telex: 40971
49 Rooms - DKK 800
Open: All year
Credit cards: All major
At Fredensborg Palace gates
Located 50 km N of Copenhagen

One of Denmark's oldest inns, the Hvidsten Kro (built in 1634), was moved to Hvidsten in 1790. It has been owned and managed by the Fiil family for over 100 years. Marius Fiil, the grandfather of the present owner, was a key organizer of the Danish resistance movement during the Second World War. He, his son Niels, his son-in-law Peder, his daughters Tulle and Gerda were arrested by the Gestapo in March, 1944. The men were executed, the women sent to a concentration camp, while his wife Gudrun continued to run the inn, stating that "I certainly lost much, but I still think that those who lost their men and their means of subsistence were harder afflicted than I". Gudrun died in 1972. Always known for its good food, the Hvidsten Kro has five cozy dining nooks set under low beamed ceilings. It is an extremely charming inn with clocks, rust-painted timbered walls hung with copper, pewter mugs, and weathered paintings, tables paired with wooden benches worn smooth by years of use, a cupboard with a handsome bottled glass cabinet door set in a corner niche, heavy old trunks, plate racks, fresh flowers and dramatic fireplaces. There are eight simple, inexpensive bedrooms, none with private bathroom.

HVIDSTEN KRO
Owner: C. A. Paetch
Mariagervej 450, Hvidsten
8981 Spentrup, (Jutland) Denmark
tel: (06) 47 70 22
8 Rooms - DKK 230
Open: *All year
* Except Mondays, Sep 15 to May 15
Credit cards: None
300-year-old inn, charming restaurant
Located 10 km N of Randers

In the 17th century King Christian IV chose this idyllic spot, on a forested peninsula almost surrounded by water, as an easily defendable site for a castle. You can see, through the trees, the copper tower roof and brick frame of the castle in the distance as you drive around the inlet at the end of Kerteminde Fjord to the castle's entrance. Impressive wooden doors with lion handles open to the tower's square entrance hall: take notice of the magnificent ceiling here, dramatic with its individually framed designs. Intimate in size, Ulriksholm Slot has lovely old rooms glimpsed through heavy wooden doorways. The dining room is regal in its decor and offers a tempting lunch and dinner menu for both residents and visitors. It was actually the chef himself who escorted us on a tour. The castle, now under the protection of the Danish Preservation Act class A, has 16 handsome bedrooms, each with a handbasin, though none has a private bathroom. The management is particularly proud of the bridal suite with its romantic four-poster bed.

ULRIKSHOLM SLOT
Owner: Anette Bastrup
Kolstrup, 5300 Kerteminde
(Funen) Denmark
tel: (09) 39 15 44
16 Rooms - DKK 400
Closed: Jan
Credit cards: All major
17th-century castle
Located 25 km E of Odense

This is a delightful inn whose popularity is evidence of the Andersen family's high standard of service since 1949. The senior Mrs Andersen has written a cookbook entitled "Inn Food", a subtle indication of the fine dining you can expect to sample here. A lovely reception area serves as a wonderful introduction to the Kongensbro Kro and a salon warmed by a fireplace sits just off the entry. Drinks and light meals are served here in this lovely room which displays a handsome grandfather clock, some primitive pewter spoons, decorative Windsor chairs and wooden benches set against the wall. Up a staircase whose banister is charmingly carved with hearts and clubs is a wing of guestrooms running the length of the hotel. Recently remodeled, these bedrooms are comfortably equipped and look out through dormer windows to the river. The Kongensbro Kro is just outside Ans, set a short distance off the main road to Viborg - a surprisingly quiet location. Its back garden slopes down to the tree-lined Gudena River, where guests can enjoy the fine fishing and can also rent canoes to explore beyond the bend in the river.

KONGENSBRO KRO
Owner: Ole Andersen
Gl. Kongevej 70
Kongensbro, 8643 Ans
(Jutland) Denmark
tel: (06) 87 01 77
16 Rooms - DKK 500
Closed: Christmas & New Year's Day
Credit cards: All major
Lovely riverside inn
Located 66 km NW of Arhus

The decor of the Fru Larsen is a delightful mix of antiques in a modern setting: heavy doors whose handles are formed from large pipes and a sienna, stucco exterior are a deceptive introduction to a cozy, warm interior. The restaurant was converted from a grocery store in 1977. Tables, lovely wooden pieces, rich in their age and patina, are set round a central fireplace and the brick floors are warmed by Oriental throw rugs. From an impressive arrangement of meats, fresh cheeses, homemade jams, warm bread and tempting pastries, breakfast is served with as much flair and colorful presentation as either lunch or the gourmet dinners. Kirsten and Flemming (who are married) are both accomplished chefs, having trained for several years in France. They pride themselves on their Franco-Danish cuisine. The restaurant is closed on Mondays. The eight bedrooms, each named after a woman whose portrait hangs on the wall, are a recent addition (1986) and are located across the street. The bedroom floors are stripped wood and the brick bathroom floors are warmed by subfloor heaters. Antiques decorate the rooms, fresh flowers are artistically set about and wood shutters block out the street lights and morning sun.

FRU LARSEN
Managers & Chefs: Kirsten Munck & Flemming Frandsen
Ostergade 1, Laurbjerg
8870 Langa, (Jutland) Denmark
tel: (06) 46 83 88
8 Rooms - DKK 600
Open: All year except Christmas
Credit cards: All major
Excellent restaurant
Located 50 km NW of Arhus

The charming Hotel Postgaarden sits on the main square of Mariager behind an old timbered facade stretching along an uneven cobblestoned street. Concerned townspeople supervised the recent restoration of this inn and elected Kurt Bjerre to manage the hotel - his efforts reflect their pride and interest. Heavy old beams, original to the house, add character to the hotel's many cozy rooms. Tea and light snacks are served at tables covered with brown checked cloths in what is the oldest part of the inn - the Vicar's Apartment, dating back to 1688. You can settle in any of the four snug dining rooms, the Marinestue, Almuestue, Mariagerstue and Jagstue, and enjoy a delightful dinner. Every third Thursday evening during the winter months you can hear local music played in what was once the old hotel salon. A corridor bounded by walls built in 1710 leads to the inn's superb bedrooms. With their light wood furniture, all the rooms are exceptional in their decor and outfitted with private, modern bathrooms. Tucked under the interesting angles of the inn's roofline, the Wedding Suite offers the most spacious accommodation. The bedrooms at the back overlook the hotel's herb garden.

HOTEL POSTGAARDEN
Manager: Kurt Bjerre
Torvet, 9550 Mariager
(Jutland) Denmark
tel: (08) 54 10 12
10 Rooms - DKK 475
Open: All year
Credit cards: All major
Timbered 18th-century inn
Located 58 km S of Alborg

Chosen for the cover of this book, the Falsled Kro is perfection in deluxe country inns. Nestled in a small farming village, this charming complex has offered accommodation since the 16th century. The most spectacular guestrooms are the three suites built in the style of a Funen farmhouse, with exposed beams, red tile floors and small paned windows. For example, room 16 is stunning: an inviting living room warmed by a large open fireplace, a spacious dining area and a bedroom whose luxuriously appointed bathroom is decorated with handpainted tiles - very expensive but worth the splurge. At dinner time you make your menu selections over an aperitif by a warming log fire before being escorted into the elegant dining room where stunning flower arrangements reflect dramatically in the patina of the gorgeous antique tables. Most tables enjoy a view through a large archway into the kitchen where a massive stove sits center stage and the chef, and co-owner, Jean-Louis Lieffroy creates delectable dishes with the assistance of numerous chefs and apprentices. A delightful breakfast is served in a bright room where whitewashed brick walls, white wooden chairs, marble tabletops and colorful tiles complete a crisp fresh decor.

FALSLED KRO
Owners: Sven & Lene Gronlykke
Chef & co-owner: Jean-Louis Lieffroy
Assensvej 513
5642 Millinge, (Funen) Denmark
tel: (09) 68 11 11
14 Rooms - DKK 980
Open: Mar 1 to Jan 1
Credit cards: AX, DC
16th-century thatched inn
Located 50 km SW of Odense

With a history that dates back to 1310, the Steensgaard Herregardspension has had many colorful owners: one supposedly hired her cook to bludgeon her husband to death with a cleaver - she still "haunts" the room where her husband was murdered, trying in vain to scrub his blood off the floorboards. Over the years the manor has been extensively expanded and remodeled, and became a hotel only 30 years ago. The decor is rich and regal, with handsome fireplaces, decorative wainscoting, intricate inlaid floors decked with Oriental carpets, dramatic fresh flower arrangements, a sweeping staircase and beautiful furniture in all the rooms. Of the bedrooms, number 7, the Count's Room, is a most impressive double, decorated in red velvet, with its own steep narrow stairway leading to the second floor. Room 15 is an especially attractive corner double, decorated in salmon tones and enjoying a large private sitting area, but lacking a private bathroom. Guests can enjoy a wide range of recreational facilities, some of which are symbolized in the house coat of arms: riding, hiking in the forest and angling are represented by a horse, a tree with squirrels, and a fish. The hotel also offers billiards, croquet and tennis.

STEENSGAARD HERREGARDSPENSION
Owner: Peter Hansen
Manager: Bent Lillemark
5642 Millinge, (Funen) Denmark
tel: (09) 61 94 90
15 Rooms - DKK 650
Open: Mar 1 to Jan 1
Credit cards: EC, AX
Riding, billiards, tennis, croquet
Located 50 km SW of Odense

Odense is a lovely city and a popular destination for visitors, primarily because Hans Christian Andersen was born here. The Golf Plaza Hotel is conveniently located on the main road that circles the city (across from the east train station). Only a few minutes' stroll from the hotel is the center of the old city where you will find Hans Christian Andersen's house, the theater and the pedestrian shopping thoroughfare. The hotel lobby is dramatic, looking up to a lovely, open and circular Fairytale Gallery. Lounge chairs are set around the gallery banister, a perfect place to read or watch who comes and goes from the hotel. Most of the bedrooms are furnished in the original formal style, while a few others have a traditional modern decor. The Rosegarden, with its exquisite handmade leather furniture, is considered to be one of Denmark's finest gourmet restaurants. A bountiful Danish buffet breakfast of rolls, a selection of cold meats, poached eggs, yogurt, juice and coffee is offered in a bright sitting room. Since this hotel is owned by a corporation, although efficiently and caringly managed, do not expect the atmosphere characteristic of an owner-operated inn.

GOLF PLAZA HOTEL
Manager: David Bone
Ostre Stationsvej 24
5000 Odense C., (Funen) Denmark
tel: (09) 11 77 45 telex: 59471
70 Rooms - DKK 730
Open: All year
Credit cards: All major
Central city hotel, excellent restaurant
Located opposite the east train station

At the junction of 13 roads, Randers has served for centuries as a thriving market town and its medieval quarter with its beautiful old houses, narrow streets and pavements has been lovingly preserved as a pedestrian district. The front door of the Hotel Randers opens up to the heart of this complex, while an underground parking lot, reached from Brodregade, provides direct driving access. Once you experience the kind hospitality and welcome of the staff, it is easy to understand why this hotel recently received the American Express award for outstanding service. Built in 1856, the hotel was the first in Jutland and has been owned by the same family for over 100 years. A large comfortable lounge is a popular gathering spot and you can enjoy international cuisine in the restaurant, or a less formal meal in the grill-room or the Kahytten, the bar. For the affordable price the accommodation is excellent value: you can stay in a quite luxurious suite for the cost of a standard double room in many hotels. The bedrooms' decor varies from antique to modern: you may choose the style you prefer when you make your reservations.

HOTEL RANDERS
Owner: Sonja Mtahisen
Manager: Alex Villadsen
Torvegade 11
8900 Randers, (Jutland) Denmark
tel: (06) 42 34 22
85 Rooms - DKK 560
Open: Jan 2 to Dec 21
Credit cards: All major
Personalized service
Located 76 km S of Alborg

Important as a Viking trading center, Ribe lays claim to being Denmark's oldest town. Proud of its colorful past and beautiful old buildings, the night watchman relates Ribe's history as he follows his traditional evening rounds, between May 1st and September 15th. His "tour" begins at 10 pm from Torvet Square near the Hotel Dagmar. This old building dates back to 1581 and has been a hotel since 1850. From the main lobby a stenciled stairway leads to the oldest bedrooms. Found along a creaking, slanting corridor and tucked behind low doorframes, these 18 older guestrooms do not have private bathrooms but they are full of olde-worlde character - the front bedrooms look out across the bricked square to the cathedral. If you prefer a private bathroom, request one of the modern bedrooms located in another wing of the hotel. Wainscoting and rich tones of gold, green and red decorate the hotel's popular and busy restaurant, while the Vaegterkaelderen, the hotel's bar, is a cozy spot for a less formal meal or quiet drink. Breakfast is served in what was once the living room.

HOTEL DAGMAR
Manager: Leif G. Petersen
Torvet 1
6760 Ribe, (Jutland) Denmark
tel: (05) 42 00 33
48 Rooms - DKK 560
Open: All year
Credit cards: All major
U.S. Rep: Best Western
Rep tel: 800-528-1234
Charming old town
Located 30 km SE of Esbjerg

In 1648 Soren Anderson Weis came here from Itzehoe and built an inn offering food and accommodation to herdsmen taking their cattle from northern Jutland to Hamburg. Often, instead of paying for their shelter, the herdsmen payed with their belongings and today some of these are displayed at the inn. The Weis family owned the leaning half-timbered inn until 1915 when it was taken over by the local authority which has done a beautiful job preserving this pretty inn. The popular bar-restaurant, with its decorated beamed ceiling, dark wood panels painted with biblical scenes, farm tables, accents of brown and white Dutch tiles, a copper bed warmer, pewter plates and mugs and an old clock, is particularly memorable. A few smaller, more intimate, rooms serve as quiet niches for small groups around a clustering of one or two wooden tables and benches. Climbing up the short narrow stairway to the five bedrooms, with the assistance of the stairway's simple rope banister, is reminiscent of climbing into a loft. The floors creak, the ceilings are low and the rooms are extremely small, simple and without private bathrooms. But the price is reasonable, the furnishings are fresh and clean and an occasional antique piece and flowers set a very appealing mood.

WEIS STUE
Manager: Knud Nilsen
6760 Ribe,
(Jutland) Denmark
tel: (05) 42 07 00
5 Rooms - DKK 320
Open: All year
Credit cards: None
Half-timbered 17th-century inn
Located 30 km SE of Esbjerg

Roskilde is a lovely cathedral city that warrants a visit if only to see its spectacular museum dedicated to the memory of the Scandinavians' valiant ancestors - the Vikings. Five Viking ships have been uncovered and their skeletons reconstructed and displayed in this concrete building whose large glass windows open to the waters of the bay. The stately Hotel Prindsen is conveniently located at the city center just a few blocks from the cathedral, where many of Denmark's kings and queens are entombed. This three-story, clean, white building was completely renovated, from the basement to the attic, in 1981. Antiques are used in the hallways and the public areas while the bedrooms have clean and simple modern decor with light wood furniture and delicate fabrics. The restaurant offers a menu of both light and more elegant meals. The hotel bar is a popular meeting spot with locals and visitors alike.

Note: Just a short walk from the hotel, we discovered a charming, inexpensive restaurant, the Bodega Club 42 (Skomagergade 42, tel: (02) 35 17 64) and sampled a scrumptious assortment of traditional Danish sandwiches.

HOTEL PRINDSEN
Owner: Martin Bank
Algade 13
4000 Roskilde, (Sealand) Denmark
tel: (02) 35 80 10
41 Rooms - DKK 580
Open: All year
Credit cards: EC, DC, AX
Located near the cathedral
Located 24 km W of Copenhagen

A delightful alternative to a central hotel while visiting the Viking museum at Roskilde is the Svogerslev Kro, a charming thatched inn 6 kilometers from the outskirts of the city. The Svogerslev Kro has been welcoming guests into its cozy restaurant since 1772 and with the addition several years ago of two annexes of bedrooms the inn is now able to welcome overnight guests. The owner, Flemming Petersen, has done a splendid job with his bedrooms which with their beamed ceilings and delightful decor exactly match the mood and feel of the original thatched inn. The restaurant is the hotel's pride, its kitchen open daily from 11:00 am to 9:30 pm, except on days that private parties monopolize the facilities. The inn has proven so popular that private parties are required to book functions three years in advance.

SVOGERSLEV KRO
Owner: Flemming Petersen
Holbaekvej
Svogerslev, 4000 Roskilde
(Sealand) Denmark
tel: (02) 38 30 05
13 Rooms - DKK 350
Closed: Christmas & New Year's Day
Credit cards: DC
Excellent restaurant
18th-century thatched inn
Located 30 km W of Copenhagen

Skagen is a charming beach community on the tip of the island of Jutland. Grass covered dunes stretch out along a peninsula dividing the Skagerrak from the Kattegat where the waves from both pound together on the point. Artists and writers come to this region and particularly to this village inspired by the spectacular seascapes. Brondums Hotel, looking like a private home, sits opposite the village museum. The exterior is brick and tile, while the interior is lovely with elegant lounges where handsome hardwood floors are dressed with Oriental carpets and inviting tables and chairs are set round a large fireplace - a perfect spot for afternoon tea. An intimate dining room offers such fine food that I was tempted to stay longer and take advantage of the hotel's pension rates. Half of the bedrooms are located upstairs in the main building while the others are in an annex 100 meters away. Although most of the bedrooms are without private bathrooms (none in the main building), most have a washbasin. Airy and spacious, the bedrooms are attractive in their simple, light wood furniture. What is particularly interesting is that most of the old paintings that hang on the walls were given in exchange for room and board.

BRONDUMS HOTEL
Manager: Per Norgaard
Anchersvej 3
9990 Skagen, (Jutland) Denmark
tel: (08) 44 15 55
48 Rooms - DKK 595
Open: All year
Credit cards: All major
Seaside village
Located on N tip of Jutland peninsula

Fano is an enchanting island of thatched farmhouses detailed with rust and green trim and fronted by beautifully manicured gardens enclosed by picket fences - a real gem. Here the Sonderho Kro, a National Trust House, is set charmingly against a backdrop of sand dunes. Since its liquor license was issued on May 2nd 1722, the Sonderho Kro has always been maintained as an inn. In 1977 a wing of seven double rooms was built to exactly match the stucco and thatch of the original building: these bedrooms are each named for a particular sailing vessel and are all decorated differently. A fireplace warms the entry hall and upstairs a large residents' lounge looks out across the sand dunes and tidal flats. Tucked behind its low, arched doorway, the restaurant is most inviting with antiques, cheerful flower arrangements, old clocks, paintings and wood richly glowing with the patina of age. The inn continues the tradition of a warm welcome and hearty food, brought to your table by charming girls dressed in local costumes. The Sonderho Kro gives a real taste of old-fashioned Danish hospitality. Note: It is a 20-minute ferry ride from Esbjerg to Nordby on Fano Island, a half hour's drive from Sonderho. Schedules are limited, but information and reservations can be obtained by contacting the ferry station in Esbjerg, tel: (05) 12 00 00.

SONDERHO KRO
Owners: Olga and Erik Jensen
Sonderho
6720 Fano, Denmark
tel: (05) 16 40 09
7 Rooms - DKK 650
Closed: First Sun in Dec to Dec 27
Credit cards: DC
Charming restaurant
Located on the island of Fano

Outside the lovely city of Silkeborg in a small farming village is a dear thatched inn, the Svostrup Kro. Tucked behind an arched entry with its own enclosed courtyard, set on the quiet banks of the Gudena River, this inn was built in 1834 to offer sustenance to passing bargemen. It is the Hilsens' hard work remodeling and decorating that has converted what they found as an empty timbered shell into a charming and inviting farmhouse hotel complex. This lovely inn has only nine bedrooms, none with private bathroom - though there are plans to build ten bedrooms with en-suite bathrooms. The restaurant is charming - intimate with soft lights, candles, lovely flower arrangements and countryside paintings framed in the ceiling beams. The menu is very reasonably priced and known for its fish courses. Every Saturday a wonderful buffet is offered. At the center of the inn the tavern remains, much as it was in the days of the bargemen, filled with conversation and atmosphere.

SVOSTRUP KRO
Owners: Karin & Niels Hilsen
Svostrup
8600 Silkeborg
(Jutland) Denmark
tel: (06) 87 70 04
9 Rooms - DKK 300
Closed: Jan
Credit cards: MC
Charming restaurant
Riverside inn
Located 10 km N of Silkeborg

The story goes that in 1737 King Christian VI was passing Soholme Inn and called out to a group of harvesters who had been caught in the rain, "Take shelter in the inn", or translated, "Kryb i ly". On that day the Soholme Inn became the Kryb I Ly Kro, or inn. Tragically, the original building was burnt to the ground in 1973, but fortunately it has been rebuilt and attempts have been made to match the style and mood of the old buildings while adding more modern facilities and larger bedrooms. Because Taulov is near the bustling town of Fredericia the Kryb I Ly is a popular overnight stop for businessmen. The dining room is most attractive and has a deserved reputation for enjoyable food. An indoor swimming pool and, for a fee, a sauna and solarium are available for guests' use. Although this is a new hotel the management strives to live up to the old inn's motto "Good folk come where good folk are".

KRYB I LY KRO
Manager: Svend Erik Kristensen
Kolding Landevej 160
Taulov, 7000 Fredericia
(Jutland) Denmark
tel: (05) 56 25 55 telex: 51108
46 Rooms - DKK 800
Open: All year
Credit cards: All major
Newly rebuilt in original style
Indoor swimming pool, sauna, solarium
Located 5 km W of Fredericia

This small countryside inn was named after a knight, Niels Bugge, the owner of a neighboring estate during the 1350s whose crest is found on the sign of the inn. The Niels Bugge's Kro began life as the mill of Count Frederick Schinkel of Hovegaard, who was famous for his generosity in offering drinks to passing friends and travellers. Today, owned by the state, the inn is co-managed by Poul Nielsen and Claus Engmann and offers a fine menu in addition to a refreshing drink. The restaurant is small and very attractive, and popular with locals from the nearby city of Viborg. Accommodations are very simple and few in number: four bedrooms, none with private bath, are found on the second floor and, although plainly furnished, are very clean and quiet. Room 4, a back corner room, overlooks the lake.

NIELS BUGGE'S KRO
Managers: Claus Engmann & Poul Nielsen
Dollerup
8800 Viborg
(Jutland) Denmark
tel: (06) 63 80 11
4 Rooms - DKK 320
Closed: Dec 22 to Mar 1
Credit cards: AX, MC, VS
Popular restaurant
Small, simple inn
Located 6 km S of Viborg

Voersaa is a tiny village south of the seaside/artist town of Skagen on the northeastern coast of Jutland. The hostelry is found on the country lane that leads from the village to the coast. A Danish flag flies proudly outside the blue-green shuttered building and serves as a promise of the fine Danish hospitality offered within. Usger Jensen is often present to offer a kind welcome. There are 22 bedrooms (9 with private bathroom) found in three buildings of this 300-year-old inn, all very simply furnished. The main building houses the pub and the restaurant where low, beamed ceilings are inscribed with old Danish sayings and lace curtains dress the windows. The pub is extremely inviting and the restaurant delightful. Guests return year after year to this spot on the edge of the Voer River for fishing and boating vacations. (A few rowboats are available for guests' use.) During the summer months the hardy can swim in the crystal clear sea water from the sand banks of the Kattegat.

VOERSAA KRO
Owner: Usger Jensen
Voersaa, 9300 Saeby
(Jutland) Denmark
tel: (08) 46 00 06
22 Rooms - DKK 360
Open: All year
Credit cards: None
On the Jutland coast
Located 45 km NE of Alborg

Finland

Map of Finland Showing Hotel Locations

The name "Palace Hotel" conjures up the image of a regal old palatial hotel, yet this is not the case, for the Helsinki Palace is starkly modern. We have included it for two reasons: it has superb views of the waterfront and it has an excellent location near Helsinki's colorful market square. The entrance is on the street level where the friendly receptionist will check you in and direct you to the elevator which will whisk you to the ninth floor where all the guestrooms are located. If you choose the Palace Hotel, be sure to splurge and request one of the rooms in the front with a balcony overlooking the harbor and the market square. Although the guestrooms are simply furnished, their bathrooms are splendidly equipped with warm towel racks and an assortment of lotions and shampoos. You can rise early in the morning and stroll down the quay to watch the bustle of the early morning outdoor market where the fishermen sell their catch and flower stalls burst with brilliant color. From your balcony you can watch the impossibly large Silja Line ferries from Sweden steam by to moor just steps away from the hotel.

PALACE HOTEL
Manager: Kaarina Zeadler
Etelaranta 10
00130 Helsinki, Finland
tel: (90) 171 114 telex: 121570
59 rooms - FIM 970
Open: All year
Credit cards: All major
U.S. Rep: Best Western
Rep tel: 800-528-1234
Modern hotel - view of waterfront
Located overlooking Helsinki harbor

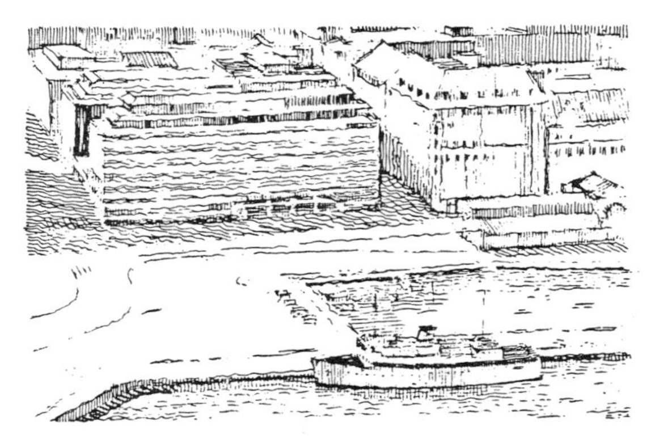

The Hotel Seurahuone Socis is very conveniently located in the heart of Helsinki just across the plaza from the railroad station. You enter a small lobby where tall marble columns lend an air of sophistication. The stairs to the right lead up to a small, very busy, cafe where tiny marble tables are set off by a line of fancy crystal chandeliers hung from the ornate plaster ceiling. Miniature balconies overlook this popular rendezvous. However, my favorite place to sit and relax is the small bar/cafe down a few steps from the lobby. This cozy little circular room is domed with an intricate glass ceiling which crowns a series of intimate tables surrounding a central fountain. Perhaps my heart was won by the total mood - a pianist playing romantic old songs from the forties and the excellent food. Only snack-style meals are served and I enjoyed delicious open-faced shrimp sandwiches. Some of the bedrooms are pleasantly furnished with dark wood, built-in Finnish modern furniture; others have painted Victorian-style wrought iron beds. Although not outstanding in their decor, the bedrooms are most satisfactory, with reading lights, comfortable beds and nice bathrooms.

HOTEL SEURAHUONE SOCIS
Manager: Martin Legercrantz
Brunnsgatan 12
00100 Helsinki 10, Finland
tel: (90) 170 441 telex: 122234
118 rooms - FIM 630
Open: All year
Credit cards: All major
U.S. Rep: Golden Tulip
Rep tel: 800-344-1212
Located in the heart of Helsinki

If you have children in tow, they will think the Messila Holiday Center is fabulous. The hotel, originally a farm dating from the 19th century, has been converted into a somewhat homespun fantasy land for children (and adults). Spreading throughout the old farm, beautifully situated on a sloping hillside above the lake, is a recreational area which includes a toboggan ride for winter or summer, horseback riding (with 30 horses available), 35 kilometers of beautiful trails through the forest, small motorized bumper-boats in the pond, Dancing Water (a large fountain whose eruption of lacy water is colored by a fantasy of lights), a sled ride with the dramatic conclusion of a splash into the water, eight ski lifts, saunas, plus swimming, boating and fishing in the lake. In addition, there are three restaurants and a handicraft center featuring a carpenter's shop, a jeweller's, a knitwear corner, a blacksmith's forge and a marvelous bakery. Here you can watch the skilled craftsmen at work and also buy beautiful handmade gifts. The old wood-frame, mustard-yellow farmhouse now serves as a restaurant, serving excellent food prepared with ingredients fresh from the farm. The one jarring note to this interesting hotel complex is the ultra-modern hotel-conference center, so when making reservations be sure to request one of the old farm cottages which have been converted into hotel rooms.

MESSILA HOLIDAY CENTER
Manager: Kyosti Toivonen
15980 Messila, Lahti, Finland
tel: (918) 531 666
45 rooms - FIM 390
Open: All year
Credit cards: All major
Horseback riding, lake, sauna
Located 104 km N of Helsinki

What a happy surprise to visit the Mukkula Manor House. The reviews I had read indicated a lovely setting, a romantic lake and a picturesque building, BUT a very simple inn with no private baths. Indeed, the pretty parklike setting has not changed, nor has the welcoming 18th-century mustard-yellow farm manor; however, this small hotel is not "basic" at all. Under the capable management of Heikki Kaija, the rooms have been completely remodeled and redecorated. Each now has its own private bath and the decor is some of the most attractive I found in all of Finland. Although not decorated with antiques, the guestrooms radiate a marvelous country ambiance. Sunlight streams through the large windows highlighting the spacious rooms with their print wallpaper, crisp-white furniture and wooden floors with a wash of blue accented by home-spun area rugs. The high-ceilinged dining rooms exude a romantic charm, with Wedgwood blue tieback drapes, wooden parquet floors, comfortable blue upholstered chairs, fine china with a blue print design and blue tablecloths. The food does justice to the decor. Not surprisingly, with rivers and lakes in every direction, fresh fish is always on the menu. The Mukkula Manor House is located beside the lake in Lahti City Park, with a sauna in a cabin by the shore.

MUKKULA MANOR HOUSE HOTEL
Manager: Heikki Kaija
15240 Lahti, Finland
tel: (918) 306 554
14 rooms - FIM 430
Open: All year
Credit cards: All major
Lake, park, children's playground, tennis
Located 104 km N of Helsinki

If you do not have time for extensive sightseeing in Finland, after less than an hour's drive east of Helsinki you can sample the countryside, combining a visit to the picturesque Porvoo, the second oldest town in Finland, with an overnight at the Haikko Manor Hotel. As you approach Porvoo by the highway, the town, with its many modern, unattractive apartments and commercial complexes, does not look too interesting, but as you cross the bridge into the old part of town, the charm is immediately evident. Colorfully painted wooden houses line the riverbank and enclose the narrow cobbled streets which climb from the river up the steep hillside. Conveniently, the Haikko Manor Hotel is only about a 15-minute drive from the village. The inn, a large white building with a porticoed entrance, has a stately "White House" facade. The parklike setting is lovely, with a large green lawn flowing down the gentle incline behind the hotel to the lake. Inside, the decor is a bit frumpy-fancy, but fun, with stately portraits peering down onto the ornately furnished lounges. The bedrooms do not have antiques, but are clean and comfortable. (There is a new, starkly modern, conference center which has been built adjacent to the hotel - so when requesting rooms, indicate you want to be in the original inn.)

HAIKKO MANOR HOTEL
Manager: Rauno Pusa
06400 Porvoo 40, Finland
tel: (915) 153 133 telex: 1734
27 rooms - FIM 660
Open: All year
Credit cards: All major
Lake, swimming pool, spa, boating
Located 50 km E of Helsinki

The Punkaharju Valtion has the honor of being Finland's oldest hotel. The idea evolved in 1803 when the Czar visited the area of Punkaharju, dotted with gorgeous lakes, and ordered that this paradise be preserved as a park. In 1845 a forester's lodge with three guestrooms was built - and so began the first inn in Finland. The setting of the hotel is superb - nestled amongst the trees on the knoll of a hill where the beauty of the lake far below can be glimpsed through the forest. A steep set of stairs cuts through the trees and winds down to the lake. The exterior of the hotel is like a cottage from "Hansel and Gretel" - a virtual gingerbread creation of beigey-pink wood siding enhanced by fancy carvings of white lacy design. The interior, however, definitely lacks the finesse promised by the sprightly facade. The main dining room is drab, although the adjacent porch-like dining room is quite cheerful, with rattan furniture and windows looking out through the trees. There are 18 bedrooms in the main building and 11 in a Victorian-style annex below the hotel near the lake. These guestrooms lack any of the touches that make a room warm and inviting, but they are clean and adequate for an overnight stay in this lovely part of Finland.

PUNKAHARJU VALTION HOTEL
Manager: Rauno Rinkinen
58450 Punkaharju, Finland
tel: (957) 311 761 telex: 5671
29 rooms - FIM 480 (5 with private bath)
Open: Jun to Sep 15
Credit cards: VS, MC, DC
19th-century forester's lodge
Located 344 km NE of Helsinki

The Hotel Rauhalinna was built in 1897 by Nils Weckman, who, in spite of being a general in the Czar's army, must have been a romantic at heart. General Weckman brought craftsmen all the way from St Petersburg to build this fabulous gingerbread Victorian creation as a gift for his wife, Alma, for their 25th wedding anniversary. Perched on a knoll with a grassy lawn running down to the lake where in summer boats criss-cross back and forth to the bustling town of Savonlinna (about 4 kilometers away), the house is a fantasy of cupolas, dormers, little balconies and intricate wood detailing - truly a masterpiece of lacy Victorian-style architecture. Inside, the ceilings are high and richly decorated and there are fancy chandeliers and lovely ceramic stoves tucked into corners. Only one bedroom, actually a suite, has a private bathroom: all others share a common bathroom in the hall. Do not expect too much from any of the bedrooms because, although some antiques are used, the overall mood is one of very dated, rather shabby decor. Nevertheless, there are very few hotels in Finland with the olde-worlde character and romance of this whimsical old building.

HOTEL RAUHALINNA
Manager: Leena Kosonen
Lehtiniemi
57310 Savonlinna, Finland
tel: (957) 253 119 Season
(957) 228 64 Off Season
7 rooms - FIM 520
Open: Jun 1 to Aug 17
Credit cards: None
Whimsical Victorian building
Located 340 km NE of Helsinki

Map of Norway Showing Hotel Locations

Kvikne's Hotel is a large Victorian creation proudly hugging the prize waterfront position on a small peninsula jutting into the Sognefjord. The hotel dates from 1887 and although a modern wing has been built, the olde-worlde original building is a like a fancy wedding cake with a white frosting of lacy balconies, wide verandas, and some antiques in the public lounges. Ask for one of the best rooms in the old section with a large balcony overlooking the fjord. These rooms are not glamorous, but pleasant with old-fashioned floral wallpaper, modern light wood furniture and attractive bathrooms. But the interior of the rooms is really of little importance because each has a wonderful view out over the fjord - views which capture the magic of Norway. Besides the romantic exterior and the spectacular views, the Kvikne's Hotel has the added plus of the Kvikne family who have inherited the art of hotel management from several generations. The enchantment remains the same: "The beauties of nature are the principal attraction. The tourists climb up the glaciers, they walk the hills or go fishing, and they visit the prehistoric grave mounds, the monuments and the old churches, or they just take it easy with a good book in the garden."

KVIKNE'S HOTEL
Owner: Per Kvikne
5850 Balestrand, Norway
tel: (056) 91 101
210 Rooms - NOK 640
Open: May 11 to Sep 30
Credit Cards: All major
U.S. Rep: Best Western
Rep tel: 800-528-1234
Fjord-front location, sauna, fitness room
Located 175 km NE of Bergen

The Augustin Hotel is the only small hotel I could find in Bergen with some olde-worlde charm. This is not a luxury hotel, so those who want sophistication should stay across the harbor at the SAS Royal. But, frankly, I loved the Augustin and will probably choose it again. The lobby is small and a little drab in decor, but with a very gracious and warm reception. The lounge is a fussy Victorian-style room on the third floor. The breakfast room is also on the third floor and a real winner, with Wedgwood blue walls, white bentwood chairs, lacy white curtains, white hanging lamps and fresh flowers. By all means ask for one of the guestrooms overlooking the harbor, if possible a corner room. Our small room, 503, had two rather frumpy overstuffed chairs, a small writing desk and brass headboard. The bathroom was not very pretty, but quite adequate: its shower had no divider, but a curtain drew across the room and miraculously kept the room dry while the water was on. What made me fall in love with our snug little room was the view: the windows are low and while lying in bed you can watch the colorful parade of ships wind their way down the fjord and into the harbor.

AUGUSTIN HOTEL
Owner: Egil Smoeraas
C. Sundtsgate 24
5000 Bergen, Norway
tel: (475) 23 00 25 telex: 40923
38 Rooms - NOK 636
Open: All year except Christmas
Credit Cards: VS, MC, AX
U.S. Rep: Scantours, Inc.
Rep tel: 213-451-0911
Located in central Bergen near the harbor

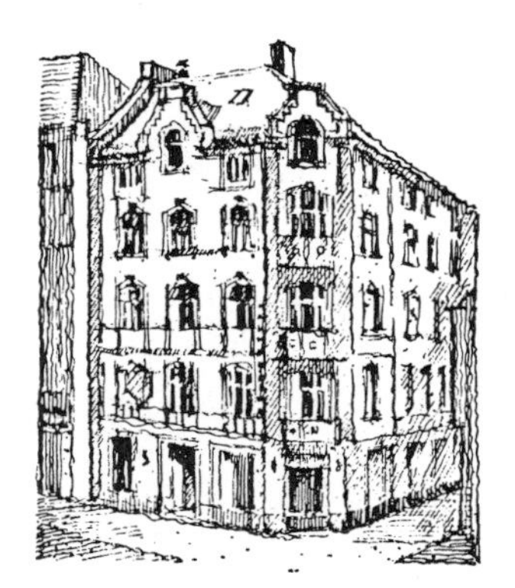

The SAS Royal Hotel is not a small inn, nor is it old, but it is a superb example of a new hotel built to blend into its historic surroundings. If you are looking for a deluxe hotel in Bergen there is nothing to compare with the SAS Royal. The location is ideal - right on the picturesque old wharf (Bryggen) whose brightly hued, Hanseatic wooden houses date back to the 12th century. Although a new hotel, the SAS Royal uses the front of these beautiful old wooden buildings as its facade facing the waterfront: these narrow little houses are cleverly joined to the new building by a glass-roofed garden restaurant. The new construction mimics the Hanseatic period, rising only four floors, with a roofline broken into steep gables, blending beautifully with its environment. The bedrooms are pleasant and the service excellent. If you really want to splurge, there is a "hotel within a hotel" - the Royal Club where the rooms, located on the upper floors, are even a bit more luxurious.

SAS ROYAL HOTEL
Manager: Inge Hellebust
Bryggen
5000 Bergen, Norway
tel: (05) 318 000 telex: 40 640
265 rooms - NOK 1190
Open: All year
Credit Cards: All major
U.S. Rep: Utell International
Rep tel: 800-223-9868
Indoor pool, sauna
Located on the wharf in Old Bergen

The Hotel Mundal was built in 1891 by Olaus and Brita Dahle, grandparents of the present owner. Many of the pretty Victorian hotels in Norway add on an unattractive modern wing - fortunately, not the Hotel Mundal. The building has been maintained in its original style with the same appealing atmosphere - a white Victorian frame construction with turrets and gables. But most special is the marvelous seclusion: until the summer of 1986, the only way to reach this idyllic inn was by ferry. Now a road tunnels through the mountains from the north, though boat is still the favorite means of access - and the most romantic way to approach the Hotel Mundal. This is not a slick, sophisticated hotel, but rather an inn with heart and a homespun type of charm, with an open fireplace in the lounge where everyone congregates before dinner. Each of the simple bedrooms is decorated individually. Room 115, the turret room, is the most deluxe, with a circle of windows overlooking the fjord and its own porch. My favorite, though, is Room 242, a small double room tucked under the eaves with a tiny balcony. This is a very quiet hotel and an idyllic spot to hide away and recoup in body and spirit. How heavenly to take long walks through the valley, birdwatching for more than 90 species of birds, go fishing in the fjord or rivers, or spend quiet hours curled up in the library with a good book.

HOTEL MUNDAL
Owner: Marit Orheim Mauritzen
5855 Fjaerland, Norway
tel: (056) 93101 telex: 74756
46 rooms - NOK 560
Open: May 20 to Sep 10
Credit Cards: None
Fabulous fjord location
Located 215 km NE of Bergen

Because of the strategic location of Flam, we felt that the town needed a hotel selection for the traveller who wants to spend the night there before taking the spectacular train that travels the Mydral mountain railroad or for those who need a place to rest before taking the scenic ferry ride down the Sognefjord. Luckily, we found the Fretheim Hotel. Although it is a simpler hotel than most others in this guide, it is filled with history and offers some charm. The public rooms of the inn are quite nice - cozy fireplaces, grandfather clocks, beamed ceilings and antique paintings give a feeling of welcome, also expressed by the friendly reception. The dining room is quite attractive and serves wholesome meals. By contrast the bedrooms are very plain - but clean and perfectly adequate if you are not too fussy. The hotel dates back to 1880, although in the beginning it had been a farm and also at one time a postal station. At the turn of the century the ever-sporty British found their way up the long Sognefjord and discovered the incredible fishing at the small village of Flam. Subsequently the Fretheim Hotel emerged to provide a comfortable place for these tourists to stay.

FRETHEIM HOTEL
Manager: Hans Thorrud
5743 Flam, Norway
tel: (056) 32 200
84 rooms - NOK 670
Open: May to Oct
Credit cards: AX, VS
On the Sognefjord
Only approach by boat or train
Located 137 NE of Bergen by train

The Elveseter Hotel is an extremely attractive mountain hotel cleverly incorporated into a very old wooden manor farm, the farm complex being grouped around a large central courtyard in the traditional style of the Gudbrandsdal Valley. Great care has been taken in the reconstruction to maintain the original peasant farmhouse atmosphere. The lounges are delightfully decorated with exceptionally fine country antiques: wedding chests, grandfather clocks, painted cupboards, leather saddles (made into chairs) and gleaming copper pots. Although the ambiance is very rustic, the amenities are conveniently modern: the various farm buildings are linked by heated corridors and each of the guestrooms has a private bathroom. There is even a large indoor pool built in the 400-year-old barn. The Elveseter family has owned the farm for five generations, and, in accordance with the old Norwegian custom, has taken its name from the farm. They have been not only farmers, but also renowned craftsmen, clock-makers and wood-carvers. Ommon, the great-great-grandfather, using the simplest of tools, turned out 104 clocks, 2 of which can still be seen at the hotel. Records show the land has been a farm for over one thousand years and the oldest building now standing dates back to 1640 - beautifully preserved by the dry, pure mountain air.

ELVESETER HOTEL
Owners: Elveseter Family
2689 Elveseter, Lom, Norway
tel: (062) 12 000
90 Rooms - NOK 460
Open: Jun 1 to Sep 27
Credit cards: None
Indoor pool, old farmhouse
Located 348 km N of Oslo

The Roisheim, located in a glorious narrow valley south of Lom, is a superb tiny hotel. I fell in love with it immediately. The hotel has tremendous character, being incorporated into a 17th-century farmhouse complex of dark log buildings topped with sod roofs. The guestrooms are very simple (only a few have private baths), but they are extremely appealing, with a country-fresh ambiance created by the use of Pierre Deux-type fabrics, wood planked floors displaying simple rugs, and painted beds topped by plump comforters. One of the oldest cottages even has its own fireplace. The lounge brims with warmth and good cheer - nothing sophisticated; just a comfortable homey collection of furniture and some country antiques around a giant fireplace. The dining room is beautiful with antique chairs stripped to their original light color, tables covered with fine linen tablecloths set with gleaming silver and flickering candles. The greatest assets of the Roisheim are Unni and Wilfried Reinschmidt. They have recently bought this little inn and their warmth and friendliness permeate the air. Wilfried adds a special bonus: he is a gourmet chef. We felt quite smug to have "discovered" this beautiful, isolated little gem, so imagine our surprise when Crown Princess Sonja and a group of friends appeared in the lounge after a day of hiking.

ROISHEIM HOTEL
Owners: Unni & Wilfried Reinschmidt
2686 Lom, Norway
tel: (062) 12031 or 12151
25 Rooms - NOK 550
Open: Feb 15 to Oct 31
Credit Cards: VS, MC
Very old farmhouse
Located 340 km N of Oslo

The Hotel Bristol is only one block from Oslo's famous shopping street, Karl Johansgate - right in the heart of Oslo. This hotel brims with character. Outside the steeply stepped gabled roof presents a most attractive picture, while inside huge columns supporting a series of arches frame the central lobby. Appropriately called the Winter Garden, this area of the hotel has a real garden effect with huge palms set amongst large leather sofas. The bar is also incorporated into this area and is one of the most unusual and attractive I have ever seen. Intimate cozy sitting areas are formed by bookshelves which create a series of individual nooks, each filled with books, soft lighting, mellow wood panelling and antique paintings. The Bristol Grill (one of several dining rooms) is also appealing with an olde-worlde hunting lodge atmosphere created by the combination of dark woods, hunting trophies, colorful plates and hunting scenes on the walls. The food must be excellent, for the chef frequently caters for royal functions at the nearby palace. The bedrooms are spacious although a little old-fashioned in decor, but, according to the hotel, loyal guests don't want to have anything changed.

HOTEL BRISTOL
Manager: Jens Brock
Kristian IV's Gate 7
0164 Oslo 1, Norway
tel: (02) 41 58 40 telex: 71668
143 Rooms - NOK 1140
Open: All year
Credit Cards: All major
Located in central Oslo

The elegant, turn-of-the-century Hotel Continental maintains a friendly, small-hotel atmosphere in spite of having 179 rooms. The hotel was founded in 1860 by Caroline Boman, a poor young Swedish girl who vowed that she would not die poor. She married Christian Hansen, a poor young Oslo man, and they went to work at Oslo's Grand Hotel. The end of the story is self-evident. Somehow, with dreams and hard work, they managed to buy the Continental - today one of Oslo's finest hotels - and Caroline Boman died a wealthy woman. Today the hotel is owned by her granddaughter, Ellen Brochmann, whose daughter, Elisabeth Caroline, will carry on the wonderful family success story. But even if my heart were not captured by its colorful history, the Hotel Continental would be a real winner just for its fabulous location. The hotel is situated in the heart of Oslo, adjacent to the National Theater and within easy walking distance of the sights and shops. The wharf, where the tour buses and tour boats depart, is only a two-minute walk from the hotel.

HOTEL CONTINENTAL
Owner: Brochmann Family
Stortingsgaten 24-26
0161 Oslo 1, Norway
tel: (02) 41 90 60 telex: 71012
179 Rooms - NOK 1200
Open: All year except Christmas
Credit cards: All major
U.S. Rep: Leading Hotels of the World
Rep tel: 800-223-6800
Located in the heart of Oslo

The Gabelshus Hotel is a good choice for Oslo if you do not want to splurge for one of the more deluxe hotels that we recommend. The Gabelshus is not a budget hotel, but for the expensive city of Oslo, it is a bargain. The location is not perfect - a brisk 15-minute walk to the heart of town - but just near the hotel either a trolley or a bus will quickly take you into the city center for sightseeing and shopping. The three-story hotel with its mansard tiled roof is not very old but quite attractive, with a lawn in front and ivy creeping over the red brick facade. The interior is definitely olde-worlde, with a cozy English country house ambiance. An especially attractive room is the lounge to the left of the reception area. Here white walls, a panelled ceiling, a fireplace flanked by old wooden chairs, gleaming copper knick knacks and bouquets of flowers create a very homey atmosphere. The guestrooms are pleasant, although with a modern, motel-like appearance. There is a large dining room, light and airy, with big windows looking out into the back garden. The Gabelshus is definitely a hotel with personality, quite different from any other in Oslo. If you don't mind being away from the town center, this might be just the hotel for you.

GABELSHUS HOTEL
Manager: Agathe Riekeles
Gabeles Gate 16
0272 Oslo 2, Norway
tel: (02) 55 22 60
45 Rooms - NOK 860
Open: All year except Christmas & Easter
Credit cards: VS, AX
About 15-minute walk to city center
Located in a residential area of Oslo

The original part of the Holmenkollen Park Hotel is most interesting - a red log building with high fancy steeple and gabled roof with dragon-like designs. The effect is of a cross between a Viking ship and a stave church. The "Viking" part of the hotel is fabulous: an antique-filled dining room and a series of small conference rooms. The tastefully decorated bedrooms are in the new wing that stretches out to the left of the hotel. Those in front are more expensive, but well worth the price - the view is sensational. A gaudy modern lobby joins the two sections together. The Holmenkollen Park Hotel is located near Oslo's famous Holmenkollen Ski Jump. There is a free shuttle bus which leaves every hour for Oslo, and a short walk down the hill there is a wonderful antique wooden trolley which makes frequent runs to the city. Jogging paths radiating from the hotel (used for cross country skiing in the winter), a sauna, solarium and swimming pool make the Holmenkollen Park an ideal choice for those who prefer a resort hotel near Oslo.

HOLMENKOLLEN PARK HOTEL
Manager: Ivar Hasselknippe
Kongevein 26
0390 Oslo 3, Norway
tel: (02) 14 60 90 telex: 72 094
192 Rooms - NOK 1220
Open: All year
Credit cards: All major
U.S. Rep: Preferred Hotels
Rep tel: 800-323-7500
Swimming pool, sauna, fabulous views
Located in the suburbs of Oslo

The Walaker Hotel has been in the same family since 1690 - it has been variously an inn, a posting station, a village shop and a bakery. The family tradition is richly maintained: Hermod Walaker is the cook, Oda Walaker the receptionist, the two sons waiters and gardeners, the two young daughters babysitters. The hotel is actually several buildings - one of which is a very plain 1940s-style motel cottage complex. But do not judge by this addition, because the main house is cozy in a Victorian way with beamed ceilings, open fireplace, red walls, green floor and lacy white curtains. This is where the family keeps its old furnishings and where guests frequently gather to sing around the piano. The guestrooms are very simple without any decorator touches. The location of the Walaker Hotel is enticing - just steps from the Sognefjord where small boathouses, brightly painted in reds, yellows and blues, reflect in the mirror-like water. Just across the fjord, easily reached in 15 minutes by boat, is the small, beautiful Urnes stave church - the oldest stave church in Norway. If you are looking for sophistication or elegance, this hotel would not be your "cup of tea", but if you want to find a family-style inn, rich with genuine warmth and hospitality, the Walaker Hotel has much to offer.

WALAKER HOTEL
Owners: Oda and Hermod Walaker
5815 Solvorn, Sognefjord
Norway
tel: (056) 84 207
23 Rooms - NOK 540
Open: May 1 to Oct 1
Credit Cards: None
Fabulous fjord location
Located 235 km NE of Bergen

The Stalheim Hotel dates back to the last century when it served as a stopping point for the postal service and travellers making their way through the strategic pass that joins Voss to the Sognefjord. Now tourism is the magnet which draws guests from all over the world. The original wood-frame Victorian-style hotel is long gone, lost to fire, but the present hotel incorporates the same hospitality as its predecessor. The setting is on a high bluff and the view, overlooking the valley far below, is truly spellbinding. Usually we recommend small inns, with an antique ambiance. This is a large hotel, but so unique, so awesome in its location and view, that it cannot be ignored. And, even though the building is a modern structure, the owner, Mr Tonneberg, is an avid collector of antiques. Fortunately he has incorporated many of them into the decor of the hotel. Wonderful chests, beautiful cabinets, ceramic painted stoves, antique clocks, Oriental carpets are just a few of the artifacts which add such warmth to the mood of the hotel. And even though tour groups make up the bulk of the guest list, the hotel is so beautifully managed that the individual traveller is made to feel very special. You must make reservations far in advance and, when doing so, splurge and ask for a room with a view - it's one you'll never forget.

STALHEIM HOTEL
Owner: Kaare Tonneberg
5715 Stalheim, Norway
tel: (05) 520 122 telex: 40536
130 Rooms - NOK 680
Open: May 5 to Sep 10
Credit cards: All major
On bluff above a beautiful valley
Located 120 km NE of Bergen

Ulvik is a tiny town located at the tip of a narrow branch of the beautiful Hardangerfjord. I first visited Ulvik 12 years ago, fell in love with the area, and vowed to return. Since then I've been back several times and the magic is always the same. Recommended as a place to stay is the Brakanes Hotel, hugging the waterfront at the tip of the fjord. The Brakanes, dating back to 1860, originated as an eight-room coaching inn. With the influx of tourists, the inn grew into a beautiful, very popular, Victorian-style hotel. Unfortunately, the quaint old inn was demolished in 1940 by gunfire from a German boat in the harbor: luckily everyone in the hotel was able to escape from the flames, although the hotel had to be entirely rebuilt. The new hotel is modern and does not have the original charm of its predecessor, but it does have the same view. And the panorama is truly breathtaking - one of the finest in all of Norway. So even though the hotel seems a bit slick and commercial, and even though the lobby might be bustling with tour groups, the hotel is too special not to include. Needless to say, you MUST have a room with a view. When you awaken in the morning and look out onto the fjord, silky smooth in the morning hush, reflecting the vast cliffs in the mirror-like water, you - like me - will promise to return.

BRAKANES HOTEL
Owner: Per-Ove Pedersen
5730 Ulvik, Norway
tel: (05) 52 61 05 telex: 42955
105 Rooms - NOK 760
Open: All year except Christmas
Credit Cards: AX MC VS
Marvelous fjord location
Located 150 km E of Bergen

Founded in 1722, the Utne Hotel is Norway's oldest inn. Undoubtedly this hotel also holds the record in continuity of ownership and management, for the same family has operated this small hotel for the last 200 years. With such a history, it is no wonder that the Utne Hotel is very special. The small white frame hotel sits snugly in its own little garden across from the pier where ferries constantly glide in and out - a most convenient location for exploring the Hardangerfjord. From the moment you enter, the snug ambiance envelops you in the cozy little lounges filled with antiques. My favorite room is the reception room, formerly the kitchen, with a large open hearth in the corner, a grandfather clock, antique country table - all accented by old wooden boxes, copper pots and beautiful old candlesticks. There are only 24 guestrooms, each varying in size and decor as befits such an old inn. The decor in the bedrooms is simple and old-fashioned, but comfortable and homey, with most having a small bathroom tucked into a corner or closet. Even if this were not such an appealing inn, the delicious food would certainly justify a detour to the Utne Hotel.

UTNE HOTEL
Owner: Hildegun Aga Blokhus
5797 Utne, Norway
tel: (054) 66 983
24 Rooms - NOK 560
Open: All year except Christmas & Easter
Credit cards: All major
U.S. Rep: Romantik Hotels
Rep tel: 800-826-0015
Small village on Hardangerfjord
Located 40 km S of Voss

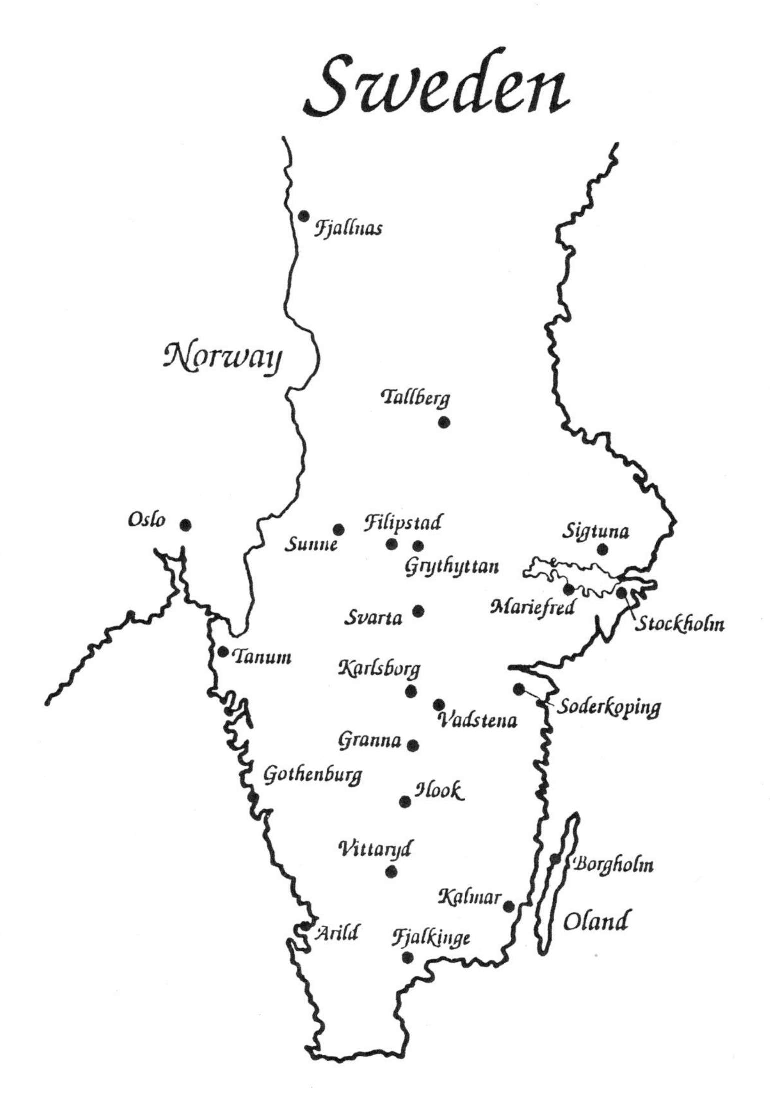

Map of Sweden Showing Hotel Locations

The Hotel Rusthallargarden is located in the charming small fishing village of Arild, and although it sits directly on the main highway leading into town, across the street is a terrace for enjoying the sunshine and the view. The hotel is incorporated into a 17th-century farmhouse which was converted into a small hotel at the turn of this century. Since that time it has been lovingly operated by the Malmgren family, of which Peter and Eva are the fourth generation, and they have created an atmosphere of warmth and coziness. Downstairs there are several dining rooms, including a very attractive room like a sun-porch with windows on three sides. There are many nooks and crannies where guests can linger, including an especially charming library with beamed ceiling and walls lined with books. Upstairs each of the guestrooms varies, but all are attractively decorated, many with antique beds and desks. Instead of numbers, each bedroom has a name such as Grandmother's Room, The Major's Room, and The Poet's Room. It is just a short walk down the main road to the quaint harbor lined with old thatched-roofed cottages colorfully painted in blues, reds, pinks and yellows.

HOTEL RUSTHALLARGARDEN
Owners: Peter & Eve Malmgren
Box 5
26043 Arild, Sweden
tel: (042) 46275
25 Rooms - SEK 550
Open: Jun to Aug
Credit cards: MC, VS
Tennis, sauna, swimming pool
Located 35 km NW of Helsingborg

Halltorps Gastgiveri is located on a delightful long strip of an island hugging the coast of southeastern Sweden. Although on an island, the hotel is easily reached by a spectacular long bridge which stretches across the water to the medieval city of Kalmar. The hotel is an old country manor house refurbished and situated on the main road just a few kilometers south of the town of Borgholm. The exterior still sets the mood of a simple country farmhouse, but the inside is a superb example of what can be accomplished with love and work. The hotel is owned by two families, the Forsbergs and the Weichls, whose devotion to detail and excellent taste is evident throughout the inn. Antiques artfully set the cozy mood and the hotel has a cheerful, happy air of brightness and light. The dining rooms are especially attractive with light colored walls, white curtains hanging from the deeply set windows, wooden ladder-back chairs and baskets of flowers adorning the tables. And, as might be expected, the meals served are outstanding: Mr Forsberg previously owned a restaurant and Mr Weichl was the chef at a famous restaurant in Stockholm. Both know fine food and how to present it with style. Definitely a winning combination.

HALLTORPS GASTGIVERI
Owners: Forsberg & Weichl Families
38700 Borgholm, Oland, Sweden
tel: (485) 552 50
10 Rooms - SEK 684
Open: All year
Credit cards: All major
U.S. Rep: Romantik Hotels
Rep. tel: 800-826-0015
Small farmhouse on Oland island
Located 35 km E of Kalmar

The Hennickehammars Manor, a romantic inn dating from the 18th century, is located about 2 kilometers south of the town of Filipstad. As you head south on the main road from Filipstad a small gravel road marked by a sign for the hotel leads off to the left. The road leads you through a forest and just when you think you have lost your way, a beautiful manor appears in a clearing in the midst of the trees. The setting is the most delightful aspect of this inn: there is a tiny pond beside the manor with a larger body of water, Lake Hemtjarn, in front, and the hotel is surrounded by woods with carefully marked walking paths leading off in every direction. A modern new conference center is being built beside the lake which, when finished, will probably detract from the rural simplicity. Inside, the lounges are light and airy and decorated with antiques. Some of the guestrooms are in the manor while others are in cottages on the lovely grounds, and each has a different decor. Some of the deluxe ones in the main manor are especially attractive with antique furniture. The exterior of the inn needs a new coat of paint, but inside everything seemed meticulously maintained.

HENNICKEHAMMARS MANOR
Manager: Bjorn Sandefeldt
68200 Filipstad, Sweden
tel: (590) 125 65
57 Rooms - SEK 650
Open: All year
Credit cards: All major
U.S. Rep: David Mitchell
Rep. tel: 800-372-1323
3 saunas, tennis, lake
Located 307 km E of Stockholm

While exploring the Chateau Country of Southern Sweden, you can set the mood by staying in one of the castles you will be visiting. Backaskog Slott (castle) dates back to 1130 when it was a monastery founded by French monks, built on a delightful spot between two lakes connected by a stream which ran through the middle of the courtyard. Later, during the Reformation, the monastery was dissolved and the property converted into a fortified castle. Backaskog Slott was confiscated in the 17th century by an important colonel of the king and still later became a royal residence. Today the castle is open to the public and well worth a visit to see the beautifully furnished rooms brimming with antiques and stately portraits. (If you are guests at the hotel, you can ask for a special viewing of the public rooms.) The old barn houses the hotel restaurant which serves cafeteria-style meals: however, if you are arriving late, eat before you come since the cafeteria sometimes closes quite early. There are a few guestrooms in the castle, but most are located in motel-style annexes in the forest behind the castle. However, I would recommend splurging and requesting the bridal suite in the castle: this suite has a large entry hall, a living room with windows overlooking the garden and a large, pleasantly furnished bedroom with a spacious bathroom.

BACKASKOG SLOTT
Owner: Gerhard Marz
29034 Fjalkinge, Sweden
tel: (044) 532 50
35 Rooms - SEK 695
Open: All year
Credit cards: All major
12th-century castle
Located 110 km NE of Malmo

The Fjallnas, dating back over a hundred years, is the oldest mountain lodge in Sweden. Many wonderful photographs on the walls indicate that the mustard-yellow wood-frame building looks quite similar now to how it did in the days of old. And the tourists still come for the same reason - the enjoyment of being close to nature. The hotel consists of several buildings, with the main lodge situated on a tiny peninsula jutting into the lake. The large dining room has windows on three sides looking through the trees out to the water. My favorite room is the cozy lounge where the warmth of the fire invites one to nestle down with a good book. The walls are artistically decorated with an enormously long pair of narrow skis, very old ice skates, mountain traps, bugles and guns intermixed with a large assortment of hunting trophies. The guestrooms also have the mountain-lodge look, pine-panelled, with sturdy pine furniture: Room 32 is especially nice, with a view out to the lake. Ulla and Nils Lundh are your warm and gracious hosts. Ask Nils about his fascinating hobby - he is Sweden's expert on the migration of the gigantic, beautiful musk ox. The Fjallnas is just what it is supposed to be - a simple mountain retreat.

FJALLNAS MOUNTAIN PENSION
Owners: Ulla & Nils Lundh
Fjallnas 10
82098 Tanndalen, Sweden
tel: (0684) 23031
29 Rooms - SEK 396
Open: Feb to Apr & Jul to Sep
Credit cards: MC
Lakeside, boating, swimming
Located 556 km NW of Stockholm

The Hotel Ekoxen is a splendid small hotel perfectly located just two blocks from the central station and only a few minutes' walk to either the heart of Gothenburg's fabulous shopping district or the main square. The cheerful mood is set from the moment you enter the light airy lobby whose large window is cozily draped with an attractive country-print fabric. Comfortable leather sofas and well-tended green plants complete the inviting room. There is no dining room, but at the far end of the lobby there is a bar where light meals are served. The guestrooms are also extremely pleasing in decor, with pastel colors combined with light furniture and rather art-deco pictures on the walls. Each bedroom is especially well equipped with a hair dryer, trouser press, small refrigerator, automatic phone wake-up, television set mounted on the wall and, most fun of all, beds that rise to a sitting position with a flick of a switch. Although the Hotel Ekoxen is outfitted in bright modern decor, the building dates back to the last century and until just a few years ago had a more colorful existence as a house of questionable reputation.

HOTEL EKOXEN
Manager: Hans Akerback
Norra Hamngatan 38
41106 Gothenburg, Sweden
tel: (013) 80 50 80 telex: 21993
75 Rooms - SEK 1200
Open: All year
Credit Cards: All major
U.S. Rep: Best Western
Rep tel: 800-528-1234
Located in the center of Gothenburg

If you are a lover of genuine castle hotels, Vastana Slott, open only during the summer months, is worth a detour. The castle, owned and managed by Rolf von Otter and his lovely wife, is far more like a home than a hotel, and indeed it is a home: Rolf von Otter was born here, as were many generations of his family before him. There is nothing commercial about this hotel. In fact, there are so few discreetly placed signs leading to the castle that, unless you are looking for Vastana Slott, you would never happen upon it. Once you find the road, it winds up the hill from the highway and ends in front of the hotel, a lovely white manor house with a red-tiled roof flanked by two small annexes which form a courtyard. The reception hall is on the first floor, with a fancy staircase leading to the upper level where there are a number of beautiful lounges superbly furnished with family heirlooms. There are seven bedrooms in the main building and two in the annex. Because the castle is so old, not all of the bedrooms have a private bathroom, but each is delightfully furnished with antiques. Breakfast is the only meal served at the castle, but there are several good restaurants just a short drive away. Staying at the Vastana Slott is like being a guest in a private home - of royalty, of course.

VASTANA SLOTT
Owner: Rolf von Otter
56300 Granna, Sweden
tel: (0390) 107 00
9 Rooms - SEK 555
Open: Jun to Aug
Credit cards: None
No restaurant
Wonderful castle above Lake Vattern
Located 186 km E of Gothenburg

Several years ago, the Grythyttans Gastgivaregard, built in the middle of the 17th century by order of Queen Christina, was facing destruction to make room for a parking lot. Luckily, a far-sighted gentleman saved the day by purchasing the hotel and putting Carl Jan Grangvist in charge as manager. The hotel has won the love and loyalty of many guests (including the King) and the success of this once doomed hotel is so spectacular that today the hotel owns the entire town of Grythyttan except for the village church. Carl Jan Grangvist is now not only the manager, but also an owner, and it is his attention to detail, love of antiques and exquisite taste that make this country inn so special. Although the furnishings are elaborate and the ambiance one of sophisticated splendor, the welcome is one of genuine old-fashioned country hospitality. The guestrooms vary in decor. Many are quite tiny, but even so are meticulously decorated, frequently with matching wallpapers and fabrics. Several of the bedrooms were recently refurbished in wonderful country prints from the collection of Laura Ashley who had come as a guest shortly before her death. There are several exquisite dining rooms and the food is outstanding.

GRYTHYTTANS GASTGIVAREGARD
Manager: Carl Jan Grangvist
71060 Grythyttan, Sweden
tel: (591) 14310
70 Rooms - SEK 665
Open: All year
Credit cards: All major
U.S. Rep: Romantik Hotels
Rep tel: 800-826-0015
Tennis, golf nearby
Located 270 km W of Stockholm

Hook Manor Hotel is a member of the Relais et Chateaux chain of prestigious hotels, and definitely deserves its rating of a deluxe hotel. Although this is a slickly sophisticated operation, the mood is one of friendliness and warmth. There are many beautifully decorated lounges and small sitting rooms - all filled with antiques. The dining room is on the lower level, with a wall of windows looking out onto a romantic small lake. We visited the hotel on Mothers' Day and mothers were being pampered with a beautiful meal while the children, who had finished earlier, were romping in the children's playground. This is a total resort with a nine-hole golf course, a putting green in the garden, pool and tennis courts. The bedrooms, each individually decorated with traditional furniture, are mostly located in various small annexes in the garden. The manor dates back to the 15th century and has been the home of nobles, military men, farmers and even a provincial governor. Luckily, the hotel is now the home of Barbro and Stefan Edberg who have converted this lovely old manor into a splendid deluxe hotel.

HOOK MANOR HOTEL
Owner: Stefan Edberg
56013 Hook, Sweden
tel: (393) 210 80 telex: 70419
90 Rooms - SEK 850
Open: All year
Credit cards: All major
U.S. Rep: David Mitchell
Rep tel: 800-372-1323
Golf course, pool, tennis, lake
Located 171 E of Gothenburg

The Slottshotellet is beautifully situated in Kalmar on a parklike, tree-lined boulevard just a pleasant walk away from one of Sweden's most dramatic sights, Kalmar Slott (or castle). The hotel was built in 1864 and the feeling is definitely one of the Victorian era, with many cozy little nooks enhanced by lace curtains, crystal chandeliers and dark wood furniture. In the back garden there is a pavilion with streaming sunlight and open airiness which sets a delightfully gayer mood than the hotel whose Victorian ambiance is much more somber. In summer the patio between the hotel and the pavilion is a blissful oasis of tables shaded by gay umbrellas set amongst cheerful flower gardens. The bedrooms, some of which are in the original building, others in an annex behind the garden, are all individually decorated and have varying degrees of olde-worlde atmosphere. Breakfast is the only meal served, although tea and coffee are always available - accompanied by fresh bakery goodies. When I visited, guests were sitting in the sunny garden enjoying a tempting array of pastries.

SLOTTSHOTELLET
Owner: Karin Plantin
Slottsvagen 7
39133 Kalmar, Sweden
tel: (0480) 88260
29 Rooms - SEK 665
Open: All year
Credit cards: EC, AX
U.S. Rep: Romantik Hotels
Rep tel: 800-826-0015
No restaurant
Walking distance to Kalmar Castle
Located on the coast 414 km S of Stockholm

For those who love boats the Kanalhotellet is a MUST. The hotel, a large brown Victorian mansion, is situated next to the Gota Canal. Most of the bedrooms are located in a new annex which stretches along the canal bank. From the outside, the annex is unassuming - a rather dull motel affair - but within, although simple and modern in decor, the rooms are pleasant and offer a stunning view. The wall facing the canal is almost entirely of glass and two strategically placed lounge chairs capture a magnificent panorama. The canal flows only a few scant yards from the guestrooms, separated by a narrow strip of grassy lawn. You will never need to attend another boat show. In summertime as many as 170 boats glide by each day - a fabulous display of vessels of every size and style. The Kanalhotellet has a history as romantic as its view. The hotel was built in 1894 by Anna and Johann Axelsson (grandparents of the present owner), who met at the White House where Anna was the housekeeper and Johann the butler for President Cleveland. They fell in love and Johann returned to Sweden where he built the Kanalhotellet along the Gota Canal, then sent for Anna to join him and become his wife.

KANALHOTELLET
Owners: Ann & Eric Axelsson Englinde
Storgatan 94
S-54600 Karlsborg, Sweden
tel: (505) 12130
25 Rooms - SEK 400
Open: All year
Credit cards: All major
Overlooking Gota Canal
Located midway between Stockholm & Gothenburg

Mariefred, an endearing small village, is where Gripsholms Castle (with one of the finest portrait collections in the world) is located. Luckily, this quaint village is only a short distance from Stockholm and the favorite approach is by a nostalgic little steamer which departs from the capital regularly during the summer. A perfect combination is to arrive by boat and then take the train back to Stockholm. Although many people come just for the day, try to spend the night in Mariefred if you can squeeze it into your schedule. The place to stay is the Gripsholms Vardshus (one of the very oldest hotels in Sweden - dating back to 1623) located directly on the waterfront. There is a popular outdoor restaurant at the hotel, a favorite for tourists coming for the day from Stockholm. In addition, the hotel features a beautifully furnished restaurant on the second floor where elegant decor and fine food combine to make eating a memorable experience. Unfortunately the bedrooms are drab and none has a private bathroom. However, when I was at the hotel Bengt Eriksson's son, who showed me around, said that the family is planning to refurbish the guestrooms. But even if they have not been improved before you arrive, I think you will enjoy this historic old inn set in such a wonderful old village.

GRIPSHOLMS VARDSHUS
Owner: Bengt Eriksson
15030 Mariefred, Sweden
tel: (0159) 100 40
10 Rooms - SEK 440
Open: All year
Credit cards: All major
Lakefront location
Located 82 km W of Stockholm

The town of Sigtuna is a gem - a truly beautiful lakeside town filled with colorful wood buildings lining a picturesque pedestrian street. The village is very popular with tourists who frequently come from Stockholm for the day. Sigtuna is about a 45-minute drive from Stockholm or an all-day excursion by boat (see page 34 for details). Stockholm's major airport is only about a 15-minute drive from the hotel, making this a convenient last-night stopover if you have been travelling around Sweden by car and want to spend one last night in a charming village before leaving by plane. Although the hotel is not especially charming or old, the village of Sigtuna is so conveniently located and so delightful that we wanted to be able to offer a hotel. The Stadshotellet is fairly new, having been built after the turn of the century. The dining rooms, two of which have large windows with a lovely view over the lake, are attractively decorated in a traditional style and serve most enjoyable food. The owner is very friendly and helpful. When I was at the hotel all of the bedrooms were being redecorated and the ones I saw were freshly painted and quite attractive - especially appealing were those with a view across the lake.

STADSHOTELLET
Owner: Lisbeth Wallden
Stora Nygatan 3
19300 Sigtuna, Sweden
tel: (0760) 501 00
26 Rooms - SEK 430
Open: All year
Credit cards: Most major
Charming old village
Located 40 km NW of Stockholm

Most of the inns recommended in this guide are quite small, or, if large, brimming with antiques. But although large, and with only a smattering of antiques, the Soderkopings Brunn has so many wonderful attributes that it is a "must" for inclusion. First, the location is superb: not only in the picturesque village of Soderkoping, but also only steps from the Gota Canal. Another plus is the romantic olde-worlde Victorian-style veranda which stretches across the front of the hotel, a perfect lazy destination for afternoon tea. Perhaps, though, the greatest asset of the hotel is the director, Stig Ekblad. His professional management and warm personality add old-fashioned heart and hospitality to this commercial hotel. Request a guestroom in the original section - these are called the "romantic rooms" and have much more charm than those in the new wings. Although the hotel has grown into a slick commercial operation, one easily slips back into the mood of yesteryear when Soderkoping was famous for its waters that attracted many illustrious guests to its spa.

SODERKOPINGS BRUNN
Manager: Stig Ekblad
Skonbergagaten 35
61400 Soderkoping, Sweden
tel: (0121) 10900 telex: 64262
110 Rooms - SEK 835
Open: All year
Credit cards: All major
U.S. Rep: Romantik Hotels
Rep tel: 800-826-0015
Swimming pool, sauna, Gota Canal
Located 179 km S of Stockholm

The Lady Hamilton Hotel is very special - a jewel of a hotel in the charming Old Town of Stockholm. The hotel brims with charm. From the moment you enter the lobby you are immersed in the motif of the hotel - covering the walls are pictures of Lady Hamilton, including the large world-famous portrait "Lord Nelson's Lady Love" by George Romney. In the center of the lobby a ship's figurehead of Lady Hamilton adorned in a flowing blue dress dominates the scene. This nautical theme is continued throughout the hotel and extends into the Bengtsson's other two hotels, The Lord Nelson and The Victory. The bright and cheery coffee room has captain's chairs and walls hung with embroidered pictures of old schooners. Upstairs, the bedrooms are small and charmingly decorated with antique folk art accents, including a delightfully painted hanging wall cabinet. A whimsical handpainted floral spray decorates each bedroom door and the rooms are appropriately named after flowers. Even the corridors are appealing, for here folk art paintings are artfully intermingled with antiques which include an adorable collection of children's handcarved rocking horses.

LADY HAMILTON HOTEL
Owners: Gunnar & Majlis Bengtsson
5 Storkyrkobrinken
11128 Stockholm, Sweden
tel: (08) 234 680 telex: 10434
34 Rooms - SEK 1085
Open: All year except Christmas
Credit Cards: All major
U.S. Rep: Romantik Hotels
Rep tel: 800-826-0015
Sauna and mini-pool
Located in the Old Town of Stockholm

The Lord Nelson, a wonderful narrow little hotel squeezed onto the main shopping street of the Old Town of Stockholm, was the first hotel opened by Gunnar and Majlis Bengtsson. The Bengtssons had not been in the hotel business before but they had a fabulous collection of antiques, impeccable taste and a keen knowledge of the ingredients needed for an excellent hotel. As the name implies, Lord Nelson and a nautical theme are the order of the day at this hotel. Ships' artifacts, highly polished brass and a mahogany reception counter set the mood in the lobby. Each of the bedrooms is named after a famous sailing ship and, best yet, within each guestroom there is an antique ship model. The bedrooms are not large, but bright and pleasant. A rooftop terrace overlooking the Old Town offers a delightful retreat on a pleasant day. A few years after opening The Lord Nelson, the Bengtssons renovated and converted several houses into their second hotel - calling it The Lady Hamilton after Lord Nelson's mistress. How appropriate that they have called their third hotel The Victory after Nelson's flagship.

LORD NELSON HOTEL
Owners: Gunnar & Majlis Bengtsson
Vasterlanggatan 22
11129 Stockholm, Sweden
tel: (08) 23 23 90 telex:10434
31 Rooms - SEK 920
Open: All year except Christmas
Credit Cards: All major
U.S. Rep: Romantik Hotels
Rep tel: 800-826-0015
Sauna
Located in the Old Town of Stockholm

The Malardrottningen Hotel is a yacht. When it was built in 1923 for the New York millionaire C. K. G. Billings, it was the largest private motor yacht in the world. Later it was given to Barbara Hutton, the Woolworth heiress, by her father for her eighteenth birthday. She kept her "toy" for only a few years and then, with a soft spot in her heart for the Royal Navy, gave it to the British when World War II began. The Malardrottningen was found "by mistake" in Stavanger, Norway, where it was being used as a very run-down youth hostel. Eighteen months of hard work and a fortune were spent to return her to her former glory. If you love boats, this will certainly be an enticing hotel choice for Stockholm. But, you must remember, this is a yacht. The cabins are all small - even the two largest, the Owner's Cabin and the Captain's Cabin, have miniscule bathrooms. However, the decor of polished woods, gleaming brass and blue fabrics is extremely attractive, the food excellent and the nautical ambiance very special.

MALARDROTTNINGEN HOTEL
Manager: Anders Hemberg
Riddarholmen
11128 Stockholm, Sweden
tel: (08) 24 36 00
60 Rooms - SEK 1047
Open: All year
Credit Cards: All major
U.S. Rep: Scantours, Inc.
Rep tel: (213) 451-0911
Hotel in a ship
Docked near the Old Town of Stockholm

The Victory Hotel is the third hotel opened by Majlis and Gunnar Bengtsson in the Old Town of Stockholm. Their first hotel was The Lord Nelson, next came The Lady Hamilton (Nelson's mistress) and now The Victory (Nelson's flagship). The same tradition of excellence continues: fabulous antiques, exquisite taste and meticulous attention to detail. The Victory, the most deluxe of the trio, has a nautical theme: each of the guestrooms is named after a sea captain and in each room is an original portrait of that captain's ship. In addition, Gunnar Bengtsson has amassed a collection of pictures of the captains and their wives. An added bonus is a discovery made while excavating for the sauna in the basement - the base of one of Stockholm's 14th-century towers. This exciting find delayed the opening of the hotel so that the tower wall could be carefully preserved and incorporated into the decor of the hotel. The Victory Hotel has a gourmet restaurant, the Leijontornet, named after a famous cache of silver (85 silver bowls and 18,000 silver coins) found in the very room that the dining room now occupies.

VICTORY HOTEL
Owners: Gunnar & Majlis Bengtsson
Lilla Nygatan 5
11128 Stockholm, Sweden
tel: (08) 14 30 90 telex: 10434
48 Rooms - SEK 1250
Open: All year except Christmas
Credit Cards: All major
U.S. Rep: Utell International
Rep tel: 800-223-9868
Sauna
Located in the Old Town of Stockholm

The Lansmansgarden is located just 3 kilometers north of Sunne on Highway 234. This is Selma Lagerlof country, and the Lansmansgarden was supposedly mentioned in some of Selma's famous novels which were written about this part of Sweden where she was born and raised. Selma's home is nearby and has been turned into a very interesting museum. This lovely white frame farmhouse is now a modest hotel whose beauty lies in its simplicity. The decor inside is my idea of very Swedish, with light colors, white painted furniture, lots of windows letting in streams of sunlight, touches of blue in painted doors and awnings and handcrafted rugs. Nothing is fancy. Nothing is decorator-perfect, but the effect is one of a warm welcome and comfy caring. The guestrooms are small, but attractive - most with crisp-white painted furniture and accents of color in the throw rugs, bedspreads and curtains. Several of the guestrooms are on the grounds in small red cottages. Behind the hotel a field runs down to the lake where fishing and boating can be arranged. When I was looking for the hotel, I met some Americans at the tourist office who had "happened" upon the Lansmansgarden and loved it so much that they extended their stay for several days.

LANSMANSGARDEN
Owner: Ulfsby Herrgard
68600 Sunne, Sweden
tel: (0565) 10301
30 Rooms - SEK 490
Open: May 2 to Sep 15
Credit cards: All major
Overlooking Fryken Lake
Located 358 km W of Stockholm

The Svarta Herrgard has an idyllic, peaceful setting. This lovely old manor house dating back to 1782 faces the main road with gates leading into the front garden. The reception hall is small, with walls decorated with antique armor. It is not until you go into the dining room that you discover the glorious view: here windows open onto the rear garden where a velvety lawn slopes gently down to the lake, ending with a white wooden pier stretching out over the water. A few rowboats are tied up at the dock waiting for guests who want to go rowing or fishing. Inside, the lounges and dining rooms are decorated with antiques which are rather fancy but presented in such a way as to give a feeling of homey informality. The food is excellent and every day a smorgasbord is available. When requesting a room, splurge and ask for one of the best rooms with antique decor and views of the lake. What paradise to awaken in the morning to the song of the birds and look out your window to the lake. If you enjoy walking, there are miles of trails available, or, if you want to fish, there are lakes in every direction for you to try your luck. Or, should you want sightseeing, there are old churches, glass factories and castles nearby.

SVARTA HERRGARD
Owners: Nils & Marianne Frantzen
71011 Svarta, Sweden
tel: (9585) 50003
41 Rooms - SEK 640
Open: All year
Credit Cards: AX, MC, DC
U.S. Rep: Romantik Hotels
Rep tel: 800-826-0015
Beautiful lake setting
Located 236 km W of Stockholm

Located in the heart of Dalarna (an idyllic rural area of Sweden) is a gem of an inn, the Akerblads Hotel. Near Lake Siljan, the hotel was once a farm, and dates back to the 15th century. Although the red-framed exterior of the inn blends perfectly with the other farmhouses in Tallberg, within is a delightful mix of country-style antiques and sophisticated charm. There are 45 guestrooms, all pleasant, but I recommend splurging and requesting one of the deluxe suites with antique decor and romantic canopied beds. The dining room is especially lovely, with a grandfather clock setting the country mood as you enter the room. But more important than the charming decor is the food: guests come from all over Sweden just for the meals. The kitchen is large and immaculate, with many chefs - each responsible for his own specialty. In the basement is a superb wine cellar where a stunning array of wines is artfully displayed. It is no wonder that this is such a special hotel - it has been in the Akerblad family for twenty generations (two sons are currently in hotel school intending to carry on the family tradition). Although this was originally a family farm, hospitality has always been a heritage of the family and in 1910 Grandmother and Grandfather Akerblad officially converted the farm into an inn, looking after their guests so well that even today those guests' children return year after year.

AKERBLADS HOTEL
Owners: Akerblad Family
79303 Tallberg, Sweden
tel: (247) 508 00
45 Rooms - SEK 680
Open: All year except Christmas
Credit cards: VS, MC
Sauna, whirlpool, lake nearby
Located 280 km NW of Stockholm

The most outstanding features of the Romantik Hotel Tallbergsgarden are Ulla and Bert Lindgren. Their graciousness permeates every nook and cranny of their cozy hotel, situated in the middle of the enchanting little village of Tallberg, in the picturesque area of Dalarna. The hotel is a complex of little houses and cottages. The original core of the hotel was the village schoolhouse in which the reception, dining room, lounge and several bedrooms are located. Nestled about the property is an interesting assortment of other buildings containing guest rooms: some are new but constructed in the old style; others are actually very old. My favorite bedroom is located in the old horse stall of weathered wood, now a most inviting family suite. The rooms do not have a sophisticated decorator touch, but instead maintain the homey comfortable style of the owners, Ulla and Bert Lindgren. The dining room (where waitresses wear the local costume) is especially attractive, with wood panelling, Dalecarlian scroll paintings bordering the ceiling and a large round buffet in the center of the room laden with Swedish delicacies and crowned by a large wrought iron chandelier.

ROMANTIK HOTEL TALLBERGSGARDEN
Owners: Ulla & Bert Lindgren
79303 Tallberg, Sweden
tel: (247) 500 26
50 Rooms - SEK 610
Open: All year
Credit cards: AX, MC, DC
U.S. Rep: Romantik Hotels
Rep tel: 800-826-0015
Overlooking Lake Siljan
Located about 280 km NW of Stockholm

Tanums Gestgifveri is a simple, wood frame hotel located in the small town of Tanum, famous as the site of prehistoric rock carvings. (Be sure to visit these fascinating 5,000-year-old engravings which depict aspects of life so long ago - such as warriors in a Viking-like canoe.) But even if it were not for the rock carvings, Tanums Gestgifveri would make an excellent stopover en route to Oslo. This sophisticated little inn is very pretty, with a cozy entry hall, a comfortable small bar and an especially inviting lounge with draperies and upholstery in matching soft green and pink floral prints - a rather "English sitting room" decor. The bedrooms are pleasant although not antique in decor. The bathrooms are small except in the suites (the King's Suite even has an enormous circular bathtub). Another reason to include the Tanums Gestgifveri on your itinerary is the outstanding food. Located down a small footpath from the hotel is a delightful small farmhouse-looking yellow frame building where delicious meals are served in a cozy antique atmosphere, while across the street in a small barn-red house is a second restaurant specializing in crepes.

TANUMS GESTGIFVERI
Owner: Regine Steiner Oster
45700 Tanum, Sweden
tel: (0525) 290 10
29 Rooms - SEK 815
Open: Apr 1 to Sep 15
Credit cards: VS, DC, MC
U.S. Rep: David Mitchell
Rep tel: 800-372-1323
Small indoor pool
Located 170 km S of Oslo

The Vadstena Klosters Guesthouse is located in the charming medieval town of Vadstena which is beautifully situated on the shore of Lake Vettern. As the name implies, the hotel is part of the old abbey founded by Saint Birgitta. Although the reception was not as personal as many others I experienced in Sweden, there is nothing austere about the little inn. The public rooms have warmth and charm created by the strategic placement of antiques. The bedrooms, although simple, are pleasant, with painted wood furniture and pastel colored walls. There is no restaurant, but a nice buffet breakfast is served each morning in the lounge. The cloisters are incorporated into the hotel and the arches are reminiscent of the early history of the inn as are the stone steps at the entrance - worn down through the ages by the feet of many nuns. The setting of the inn is perfect, adjacent to the lovely church designed by Saint Birgitta to her specifications· "plain construction, humble and strong". The effect is one of striking airiness and utter simplicity. From the church, a short stroll along the lake through a beautiful park brings you to the magnificent Vadstena Castle, certainly one of the most dramatic buildings in Sweden.

VADSTENA KLOSTERS GUESTHOUSE
Owner: The Birgitta Foundation
Lasarettsgatan
59200 Vadstena, Sweden
tel: (0143) 11530
25 Rooms - SEK 515
Open: Jan 2 to Dec 20
Credit cards: VS, MC, AX
13th-century monastery, no restaurant
Located 265 km SW of Stockholm

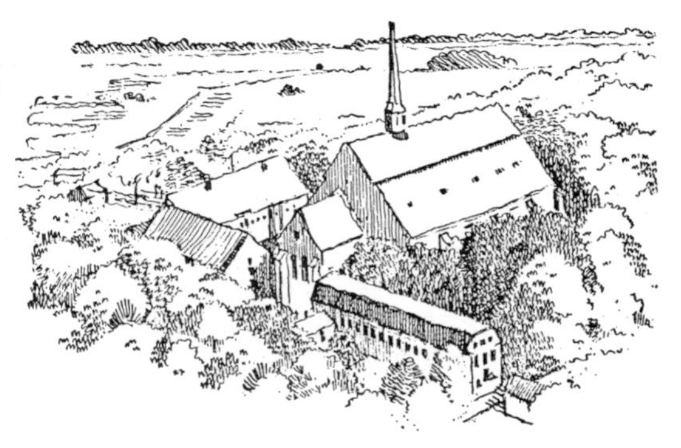

In every research adventure, a few inns remain more than a memory of pretty rooms or a delectable dining experience. Instead, sometimes we lose our hearts completely, and fall in love we did with the Toftaholm Manor House Hotel. This delightful inn is really a dream. Not just a "dream" in that it is a picturesque mustard-yellow farmhouse perfectly situated on a grassy meadow stretching out to an idyllic lake, but also a dream of its young owners, Lisbeth and Jan Boethius. When they bought the property several years ago, the old farmhouse had become dilapidated and the lake had crept up to the house in marshland. But Lisbeth and Jan saw the potential for the inn they had always dreamed of owning. They dredged the lake in front of the manor and created a beautiful green lawn rolling gently to it. They replaced the ugly modern windows with beautiful old-fashioned ones. They freshly painted all of the guestrooms, lovingly placed their antiques throughout and added fresh flowers in every nook and cranny. The result of all their efforts is a delightful inn and a dream fulfilled.

TOFTAHOLM MANOR HOUSE HOTEL
Owners: Lisbeth & Jan Boethius
Toftaholm
34015 Vittaryd, Sweden
tel: (370) 440 55
44 Rooms - SEK 570
Open: All year
Credit cards: All major
U.S. Rep: Romantik Hotels
Rep. tel: 800-826-0015
Lake, own island, boats, playground
Located 190 km E of Gothenburg

Index - Alphabetically by Town

Index - Alphabetically by Hotel

Inn Discoveries from Our Readers

Future editions of KAREN BROWN'S COUNTRY INN GUIDES TO EUROPE are going to include a new feature - a list of hotels recommended by our readers. We have received many letters describing wonderful inns you have discovered; however, we have never included them until we had the opportunity to make a personal inspection. This seemed a waste of some marvelous "tips". Therefore, in order to feature them we have decided to add a new section called "Inn Discoveries from Our Readers".

If you have a favorite discovery you would be willing to share with other travellers who love to travel the "inn way", please let us hear from you and include the following information:

1. Your name, address and telephone number.

2. Name, address and telephone of "your inn".

3. Brochure or picture of inn (we cannot return material).

4. Written permission to use an edited version of your description.

5. Would you want your name, city and state included in the book?

In addition to our current guide books, we are also researching future books in Europe and updating those previously published. We would appreciate comments on any of your favorites. The types of inns we would love to hear about are those with special olde-worlde ambiance, charm and atmosphere. We need a brochure or picture so that we can select those which most closely follow the mood of our guides. We look forward to hearing from you. Thank you.

TRAVEL PRESS – KAREN BROWN'S
Country Inn Guides To Europe

The most reliable & informative series on European Country Inns

Detailed itineraries guide you through the countryside and suggest a cozy inn for each night's stay. In the hotel section every listing has been inspected and chosen for its special ambiance. Charming accommodations reflect every price range from budget hideaways to deluxe palaces.

Order Form

If you would like to receive an additional copy or purchase other books in Karen Brown's series on European country inns, the following books can be purchased in bookstores or ordered directly from the publisher. The individual country guides are all similar in style and format. They include detailed countryside itineraries with maps and a section describing captivating hotels. These guides enhance any travel library and make wonderful gifts.

....

KAREN BROWN'S COUNTRY INN GUIDES TO EUROPE

AUSTRIAN COUNTRY INNS & CASTLES $10.95
EUROPEAN COUNTRY CUISINE - ROMANTIC INNS & RECIPES $10.95
ENGLISH, WELSH & SCOTTISH COUNTRY INNS $10.95
FRENCH COUNTRY INNS & CHATEAUX $10.95
GERMAN COUNTRY INNS & CASTLES $10.95
ITALIAN COUNTRY INNS & VILLAS $10.95
PORTUGUESE COUNTRY INNS & POUSADAS $10.95
SCANDINAVIAN COUNTRY INNS & MANORS $10.95
SPANISH COUNTRY INNS & PARADORS $10.95
SWISS COUNTRY INNS & CHALETS $9.95

Add $1.50 per copy for postage & handling. California residents add sales tax.

Indicate the number of copies of each title. Send in form with your check to:

TRAVEL PRESS
P.O. BOX 70
SAN MATEO, CA 94401
(415) 342-9117

NAME ______________________ STREET __________________________

CITY ______________________ STATE _________ ZIP _________

This guide is especially written for individual travellers who want to plan their own vacations. However, should you prefer to join a group and have all of the details of your holiday preplanned, Town and Country Travel Service can recommend tours using country inns with romantic ambiance for many of the nights' accommodation. Or, should you want to organize your own group (art class, gourmet society, bridge club, etc.) and travel with friends, Town and Country Travel Service will customize a tour for you using small hotels with special charm and appeal.

For further information please call:

KAREN BROWN'S COUNTRY INN NEWSLETTER

A Special Offering for Our Readers

Keep up with the latest happenings in the Romantic World of Country Inns. Fill out the form below and receive a complimentary copy of Karen's newsletter.

Name: ______________________________

Address: ______________________________

____

____

____

Telephone: ______________________________

TRAVEL PRESS, PO Box 70, San Mateo, CA 94401

KAREN BROWN travelled to France when she was nineteen and wrote "French Country Inns and Chateau Hotels" - the first book of what has grown to be an extremely successful series on European country inns. With ten books now on the market, Karen's staff has expanded, but she is still involved in the planning, research, formatting and editing each of the guides in her Country Inn series. Karen, her husband, Rick, and their baby daughter, Alexandra, live in the San Francisco Bay area.

CLARE BROWN, CTC, has many years of experience in the field of travel and has earned the designation of Certified Travel Consultant. Since 1969 she has specialized in planning itineraries to Europe using charming small hotels in the countryside for her clients. The focus of her job remains unchanged, but now her expertise is available to a much larger audience - the readers of her daughter's European Country Inn books. Clare lives in the San Francisco Bay area with her husband, Bill, and their younger daughter, Kimberly, who handles mail orders for Travel Press.

BARBARA TAPP is the talented young artist responsible for the interior sketches and cover painting for "Scandinavian Country Inns & Manors". Raised in Australia, Barbara studied in Sydney at the School of Interior Design. Although Barbara continues with freelance projects, she devotes most of her time to illustrating Karen's European Country Inn guides. Like Karen, Barbara shares a fondness for travel and has travelled throughout Scandinavia. Barbara now lives in the San Francisco Bay area with her husband, Richard, and their young sons, Jonathon and Alexander.